Software Testing 2020

Preparing for New Roles

OTHER TITLES FROM AUERBACH PUBLICATIONS AND CRC PRESS

A First Course in Machine Learning, Second Edition
Simon Rogers, Mark Girolami
ISBN 978-1-4987-3848-4

Advances in Mobile Computing and Communications: Perspectives and Emerging Trends in 5G Networks
Edited by M. Bala Krishna and Jaime Lloret Mauri
ISBN 978-1-4987-0113-6

Analyzing and Securing Social Networks
Bhavani Thuraisingham, Satyen Abrol, Raymond Heatherly, Murat Kantarcioglu, Vaibhav Khadilkar, and Latifur Khan
ISBN 978-1-4822-43277

Big Data: Storage, Sharing, and Security
Edited by Fei Hu
ISBN 978-1-4987-3486-8

Cloud Computing Security: Foundations and Challenges
Edited by John R. Vacca
ISBN 978-1-4822-6094-6

Developing Essbase Applications: Hybrid Techniques and Practices
Cameron Lackpour
ISBN 978-1-4987-2328-2

Embedded Software Development for Safety-Critical Systems
Chris Hobbs
ISBN 978-1-4987-2670-2

Evidence-Based Software Engineering and Systematic Reviews
Barbara Ann Kitchenham, David Budgen, and Pearl Brereton
ISBN 978-1-4822-2865-6

Foundations of Software Engineering
Ashfaque Ahmed and Bhanu Prasad
ISBN 978-1-4987-3759-3

Handbook on Session Initiation Protocol: Networked Multimedia Communications for IP Telephony
Radhika Ranjan Roy
ISBN 978-1-4987-4770-7

Healthcare Informatics: Improving Efficiency through Technology, Analytics, and Management
Stephan P. Kudyba
ISBN 978-1-4987-4635-9

Introduction to Certificateless Cryptography
Hu Xiong, Zhen Qin, and Athanasios V. Vasilakos
ISBN 978-1-4822-4860-9

Introduction to Software Engineering, Second Edition
Ronald J. Leach
ISBN 978-1-4987-0527-1

Leveraging the Wisdom of the Crowd in Software Testing
Mukesh Sharma and Rajini Padmanaban
ISBN 978-1-4822-5448-8

Machine Learning: Algorithms and Applications
Mohssen Mohammed, Muhammad Badruddin Khan, and Eihab Bashier Mohammed Bashier
ISBN 978-1-4987-0538-7

Making It in IT
Terry Critchley
ISBN 978-1-4987-8276-0

Mobile Applications Development with Android: Technologies and Algorithms
Meikang Qiu, Wenyun Dai, and Keke Gai
ISBN 978-1-4987-6186-4

Mobile SmartLife via Sensing, Localization, and Cloud Ecosystems
Kaikai Liu and Xiaolin Li
ISBN 978-1-4987-3234-5

Pervasive Computing: Concepts, Technologies and Applications
Minyi Guo, Jingyu Zhou, Feilong Tang, Yao Shen
ISBN 9781466596276

Secure Development for Mobile Apps: How to Design and Code Secure Mobile Applications with PHP and JavaScript
J. D. Glaser
ISBN 978-1-4822-0903-7

Securing Systems: Applied Security Architecture and Threat Models
Brook S. E. Schoenfield
ISBN 978-1-4822-3397-1

Software Engineering for Science
Jeffrey Carver, Neil P. C. Hong, and George K. Thiruvathukal
ISBN 978-1-4987-4385-3

Software Quality Assurance: Integrating Testing, Security, and Audit
Abu Sayed Mahfuz
ISBN 9781498735537

Speed, Data, and Ecosystems: Excelling in a Software-Driven World
Jan Bosch
ISBN 978-1-138-19818-0

The Craft of Model-Based Testing
Paul C. Jorgensen
ISBN 978-1-4987-1228-6

Software Testing 2020

Preparing for New Roles

Mukesh Sharma

CRC Press
Taylor & Francis Group
Boca Raton   London   New York

CRC Press is an imprint of the
Taylor & Francis Group, an **informa** business
AN AUERBACH BOOK

CRC Press
Taylor & Francis Group
6000 Broken Sound Parkway NW, Suite 300
Boca Raton, FL 33487-2742

© 2017 by Taylor & Francis Group, LLC
CRC Press is an imprint of Taylor & Francis Group, an Informa business

No claim to original U.S. Government works

Printed on acid-free paper
Version Date: 20160805

International Standard Book Number-13: 978-1-4987-8887-8 (Paperback)

Library of Congress Cataloging-in-Publication Data

Names: Sharma, Mukesh (Software testing engineer)
Title: Software testing 2020 : preparing for new roles / Mukesh Sharma.
Description: Boca Raton : Taylor & Francis Group, CRC Press, 2017. | Includes bibliographical references and index.
Identifiers: LCCN 2016022749 | ISBN 9781498788878
Subjects: LCSH: Computer software--Testing--Forecasting.
Classification: LCC QA76.76.T48 S533 2017 | DDC 005.3028/7--dc23
LC record available at https://lccn.loc.gov/2016022749

Visit the Taylor & Francis Web site at
http://www.taylorandfrancis.com

and the CRC Press Web site at
http://www.crcpress.com

Printed and bound in the United States of America by Publishers Graphics, LLC on sustainably sourced paper.

Contents

V

Preface

The dynamics of past, present, and future are often very profound on all disciplines, and software testing is one that has seen it all. The discipline has taken shape from very humble beginnings into one that has tremendously influenced how a product development effort is taken up. Testing processes, tools, methodologies, technologies at play (both in terms of what we test and how we test), and tester roles have all been going through a paradigm change. Having been closely associated with the software testing and quality assurance domain from the very early years, both in the capacity of a tester in a large product organization and a founder and CEO of a testing services organization, all of this has been very intriguing to me. My thoughts about the past, the present, where we are heading in the future, how all of these are interconnected, and how some elements of the past reappear are what I discuss in detail over the course of this book. My inspiration to do this at this time has been multifold:

1. We often look at the present and future, but variables from the past are equally important to consider in defining our path into the future. The current young testing crowd, especially, may miss out on this not because they do not care for the past but due to lack of consolidated information where the details are often ignored as a "thing of the past."

2. Software testing is at a very important crossroad, where we are going back to the roots on certain fronts. For instance, test automation is growing in prominence, but manual testing is becoming a niche; we are increasingly collaborating with the developers, breaking the bounds of unrealistic independence in testing, and bringing in true conscious quality. At such an important stage, it is important to take stock of the past, present, and future to define both the direction the discipline would take as well as the careers it would entail for testers.

3. I have been having in-depth discussions with several veterans in the industry, both from clients we work with as well as people who we engage with on the evangelism front. This has been a topic of detailed discussion in recent times. I wanted to use this opportunity to bring thoughts of such leaders to the forefront.

These are some of the core reasons I started working on this book in 2015. You may be aware of my earlier books on software testing: *Are You Smart Enough to Be a Software Tester?* and *Leverage the Wisdom of Crowd in Software Testing*. Both are available on Amazon. The second is also available from CRC Press. In continuation of those two books and the learnings from them, I have sequenced chapters in this book in a logical order that is easy to read, follow, and effectively impart the message. We will look at a range of topics covering where we are in the product development landscape today, what are the varied disciplines at play, what are the influencing factors bringing in a change in software testing, why is such change important, what did the past look like, what is the current decade turning out to be like, and where are we heading. As for the future, we will look at it from both near-term and long-term standpoints. We will also see in detail as to whether we, the testing fraternity, are ready to take on such changes and are empowered enough or are there gaps that we need to fill. We will talk about what all of these mean to a software tester's role and wrap it up with inputs from industry experts on what is in store for the software testing discipline and community in the coming years. I will also discuss case studies from QA InfoTech, along the way, to bring practical relevance to the points we discuss.

After reading this book, I am confident, that you as a reader, will be not just excited but also confident to take on what is in store for us in the coming years. This preparedness will be wholesome, with the required knowledge of the past and present, taking relevant elements into the future times. Once again, I am very excited to be doing this at this time, which I believe is the perfect opportunity for a topic of this nature, helping us as an industry move to the next level, influencing the change not just among us, but also at the product engineering industry level. Thanks for taking the time to read, and I look forward to your comments, thoughts, and feedback. Please feel free to write to me at mukesh@qainfotech.com.

Acknowledgments

This being my third book in the space of software testing, I increasingly believe in representing not just my experience in the books I write, but relevant knowledge of my peers, employees, and anyone from the industry who I can learn from, sharing their insights, with their consent of course. Along these lines, there are several people who have helped me get this book together in the short period of time we worked on it.

Starting with external experts from the industry, I thank Tom Churchwell, an independent test consultant who I've personally known and worked with for the last several years now; Ross Smith from Microsoft, who has supported us in all our evangelism initiatives thus far; and Rahul Vishwaroop from Adobe, our long-standing client. These are all practitioners who live and breathe quality in varied ways who have graciously shared their insights on where the industry is heading in the last chapter of the book.

My teams have contributed to case studies in the book to share their insights with practical examples in line with what I have discussed in Chapters 4 and 5. Rajini Padmanaban, who works for me handling the evangelism efforts in the company, has been closely involved from the very beginning in topic choice, flow of content, content reviews, and interactions with the publisher, among other tasks. While I call these people out specifically, I cannot not mention my gratitude to all of my employees, clients, and people from the industry that I interact with in varied capacities, who have all got me thinking from different perspectives that have helped shape this book.

I also thank Richard O'Hanley from CRC Press for taking this book up for publishing at this critical hour, when the industry really needs this topic in support of conscious, collaborative, and continuous quality. I hope you find this resource valuable in your quality repertoire and I am happy to have any further discussions with you on this topic at mukesh@qainfotech.com.

1

PRODUCT DEVELOPMENT LANDSCAPE TODAY

Everyone has their own calling, but not everyone is looking for the phone, or either they missed the call, or just not answered it.

—**Anthony Liccione**[1]

This quote applies not just to individuals but also to organizations and industries at large. Software has become omnipresent. Companies are branching into untested territories to take on new challenges and bring in unforeseen solutions. Google, for example, has multiple such projects including Google X, Fiber, and Calico all focusing on diverse portfolios from Google's flagship products around online search, advertising, and mobile operating system. The parent company, Alphabet, was formed in August 2015 to bring together the multiple brands it encapsulates into this umbrella (Figure 1.1). Google has been traditionally known to support an open culture to innovate. Twenty percent of every employee's time is set aside to innovate. Such innovations help individual employees and the organization remain nimble and dynamic that have become their imperative characteristics for staying competitive in today's marketplace.

Organizations are beginning to understand that such dynamism does not mean randomization and overwhelm, which were some of the core reasons they have often resisted big changes in the past. They are increasingly able to bring in the right focus needed for their core businesses yet focus on futuristic trends. This is a very positive outlook for the software industry at large.

Besides understanding how product development landscape today is, the other key trend to note is how global it has gotten to be. A few years ago, globalization largely meant only one of

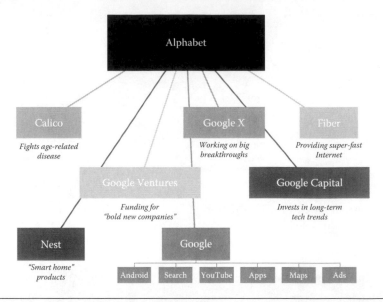

Figure 1.1   Google's organizational structure as of 2015. (From Kelly, H., Meet Google Alphabet—Google's new parent company, http://money.cnn.com/2015/08/10/technology/alphabet-google/index.html?iid=EL, 2015; CNNMoney; Company filings.)

the following three aims—for product companies from the West (especially North America):

1. Making their solutions available for global consumption.
2. Outsourcing one or more of their development needs (such as development, testing, support) as service requirements to developing countries that had the talent and less cost. This would include reaching out to countries such as India and China to get the work done offshore.
3. Setting up global development centers, again to leverage the global talent and low costs.

While this is not untrue even today, the welcoming trend is that the growth of local product companies is on the rise. Alibaba, for instance, is an e-commerce giant in China today. Flipkart and Snapdeal are making the market competitive for global leaders like Amazon in India. InMobi is competing with the Googles of the world. A number of product start-ups are being funded and homegrown, including people returning to their home countries to be a part of such revolutionary changes.

How have all of these impacted the traditional product development cycle and landscape that we have gotten used to? As a "fraternity" in the software development world, we have all come to accept the downsides of the traditional waterfall life cycle, especially its alignment with today's requirements. While there were a lot of "teething" and acceptance issues for the agile life cycle in the early 2000s, the industry has learned to implement agile in varied shapes and forms to meet specific needs. Organizations have gone agile, teams have learned to practice it to promote better collaboration with focus on result and end product, and users have started increasingly involving themselves in the software they consume even when it is still under development.

However, the question we now need to answer is, "Are these changes sufficient to meet the current needs of dynamic and global development?" The industry as a whole is attempting to answer this at this time and simultaneously take on newer practices to keep pace with the latest and greatest in the development landscape. The following are some noteworthy evolutions:

1. *Develop a user-centric and service-oriented development model*: Products and applications are no longer being built with a one-sided approach of handing a deliverable to the end user. Organizations are increasingly adopting a user-centric approach in looking for value-added opportunities to exceed end-user expectations. The whole focus of the product development effort is now on user satisfaction, thereby taking in a service-oriented approach. Thus, even a product company now brings in a service focus that further makes them more nimble and amenable to end-user wants. Users are closely involved in the development cycle, be it to review designs, evaluate the product implementation before market release, and provide inputs for future implementations, making it all a very tightly coupled development effort despite how geographically far reaching the market may be.

2. *Adopt a hybrid development methodology*: When teams started moving into the agile life cycle in the early 2000s, one of the main troubles they had was the rigidness and lack of complete

alignment to any one given model. While certain aspects of a scrum implementation may work for them, they may not be able to embrace it fully. Similarly, they may better align to specific characteristics of other models such as Kanban and XP. Over time, teams have started understanding the value of hybrid development methodologies, where they take the best of varied life cycles and create a custom model that works the best for them. Such a hybrid implementation has become an inevitable need of the day to focus on the deliverable that they are building as opposed to the rigidity of implementing a specific development methodology.

3. *Build cross-functional teams*: These are teams that run horizontal across product groups. Building and maintaining cross-functional teams continue to be a chicken and egg issue over time. In the days of the waterfall model, special functions such as performance, localization, and security, especially in software testing, were cross functional, since people with such skills were not very easy to hire, demanded high pay, and were not needed throughout the development life cycle. With the advent of agile, they had enough tasks to take on throughout a release that they were seen as resident experts in specific teams. However, cross functional has a new meaning in recent times. These experts are again being leveraged across teams given the know-how they bring to the table. Additionally, there is so much cross functionality between product teams that needs to be leveraged over the course of development—whether this is cross functionality from a product, process, or resource standpoint, organizations are looking at collaboration at all possible places and encouraging teams to become cross functional. This also helps them develop a strong sense of appreciation for the larger product context instead of looking at the specifics of a module or application they may be working on.

4. *Increased use of APIs*: This is seen as an upcoming trend. In the software world, we are not new to APIs. But what is becoming increasingly popular in the cross sharing of APIs? There is so much public knowledge and implementation available such that software systems are becoming increasingly API centric, leveraging such existing knowledge sources.

Researching for such existing reusable snippets of code will become more valuable, given how time and cost constrained teams are. Despite the value it holds, most teams often fail to leverage such common resources, even within the same organization—this is often due to lack of due diligence from their end. The ones that will differentiate themselves in delivery and implementation will be the ones that increasingly use APIs both developed at their end and also leveraged from external sources.

5. *Embrace open source*: A long-standing debate in the software world continues to be "proprietary or open-source." While this question will continue to prevail, the answer to which is very specific to an organization's individual requirements, the debate is easing out in favor of the open-source world. In addition to the cost-effectiveness and vast community knowledge open source brings in, it is also becoming increasingly sophisticated in its feature set and quality, in recent times, giving proprietary software a good run for money. In a recent panel discussion we moderated at the Next Generation World Testing Conference, this debate was taken up. Interestingly, more than each group taking its own side, they were seen touting the benefits of the other side. For example, the commercial tool vendors, such as the ones from IBM, were talking about their contributions to the open-source world, whereas the open-source proponents were talking about using commercial tools to develop open-source software to ensure robust quality. The panel was moderated in favor of a collaborative existence, although at a large level, most teams are using open source in possible places. Open source builds on their agility and productivity, without any bureaucracy around approvals. Given that open source is also soon catching up on its quality, comprehensive feature set, and the range of functions it offers, it is certainly a time to embrace it, in development efforts.

6. *Integrate individual modules into a wholesome ecosystem*: The industry as a whole is moving to an ecosystem mode. While individual modules have their own relevance, the industry has started acknowledging the benefits of an ecosystem. To take a simple example, we need no introduction to the

social, mobile, data analytics, and the cloud computing environments. However, a new technology around an integrated system called SMAC combining the four to bring in better business and user value is on the rise. Synchronizations between modules and individual systems such as these will only continue to grow, forcing development teams to think at a wholesome scale.

7. *Understand DevOps end to end*: In the integrated work that has become necessary in the development landscape, teams have come to appreciate the need for DevOps. However, they have only partly understood what DevOps stands for. While they see the piece of integrating development and operations, they still do not fully see the cultural shift that is needed to embrace DevOps comprehensively. How software quality fits into DevOps, the kind of tools that support this implementation, the team level collaboration that is needed to practice this concept in its entirety are all still loose ends that the industry will tie up together in the coming years.

8. *Secure systems*: While cross collaboration and integration has a lot of benefits to offer, it certainly opens up a whole new problem around application security. A number of touch points between systems directly translate to the number of vulnerabilities the system is exposed to. Hackers are smart in leveraging newer vulnerabilities by the day that the software development team has to increasingly focus on hardening the system and closing varied threat entry points. In the coming years, securing systems will be an important element of the development landscape.

9. *Focus on improving application performance*: Global user base for products and applications is on the rise. Obviously, this means more users are using the product round the clock. Digital consumption across the world has gone up significantly, where development efforts need to specially focus on application performance. This also includes the scalability of the underlying system that supports the application, server side performance, client side performance, and greater focus on capacity planning to ensure seamless availability all around. Thanks to advancements in technology and infrastructure, especially

in the space of cloud computing, performance is improving and keeping pace with the growing user base. However, this level of focus should continue to rise in the coming years for organizations to have a competitive edge in the marketplace.

10. *Strengthen online identification*: A great application may miss market presence because it is not able to connect with its relevant and target users. Similarly, a substandard application may pass off with a decent acceptance given its right reach with end users. Herein, the importance of search engine optimization needs to be emphasized where development efforts need to account for the right presence and optimization even as the product is being engineered.

11. *Develop collective ownership for quality*: Although the tester is still responsible for overall product quality, product teams are taking on responsibility for quality in possible ways. For instance, developers are taking on unit testing, build engineers are leveraging automated sanity tests, and everyone is interested in defects reported from the field. These are all good signs allowing testers to focus on bigger and newer tasks related to quality, enabling the team to achieve the required test coverage within the short release cycles they have to work with.

Development landscape, although agile in its implementation, will have to accommodate these evolutions into its fold, at this time. You may have already been using one or more of these evolutions, but these put together form an important set for constructively shaping your development landscape in the coming years. When teams are able to bring these into their scaffold, they are able to reap a shortened development cycle, cost-effective development approach, global reach, user connect, and a technology advantage, all of which together will be able to differentiate them from their competitors.

Roles in a Product Team

A multitude of functions come together in building a product. Roles associated with these functions are diverse and each has its own significance. Traditionally, regardless of the development methodology used, the core roles in a team that are instrumental in building a product include the designer, the developer, the tester, the build engineer, and the product manager. These are time-tested roles that have existed since the inception of software development although the functions they perform have been subjected to change over time. For example, around the late 1990s or early 2000s, the concept of independent testing was not very popular. A developer would himself or herself take on the testing and a tester would at the most come in later in the game, just before release, for a round of acceptance testing. While in the later years independent testing became popular, we are again in a phase now where everyone collectively owns quality. The tester is still responsible for quality and issues if any, but the team as a whole understands its role in contributing to product quality in possible ways. Figure 1.2 is a simple view of how software testing as a function has evolved over time. Other disciplines have also undergone similar such transformations, to align themselves with the need of the day.

Today, in line with market needs, the major roles in a software development team continue to be those of a product owner, a project manager, a technical lead, a developer, a tester, a UX designer, an architect, and a build and operations engineer. Each of these roles further has its own specializations. Specifically in the context of the

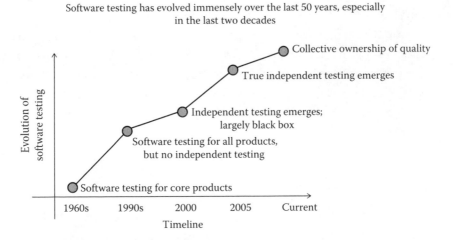

Figure 1.2 Evolution of independent testing.

testing, a tester could be any one or more of the following types: manual functional, automation, performance, localization, usability, and security. Such specializations continue to build a niche for the individual as well as the role they play all together strengthening the product under development. Additionally, a tester has to extend his or her function beyond what the core testing job entails. He or she has to collaborate with the developer, designer, build engineer, and others on the team to take on a bit of their tasks as well; for example, how can the tester take on unit testing, what kind of design suggestions can he or she provide, and how can he or she help the build and operations engineer debug issues from the field are all new factors testers that are starting to pay heed to.

With time, some of these roles may split or merge again either at an industry level or at an individual organization level, mostly driven by the needs of the product. For instance, recently, an acquaintance of mine, who has been into quality engineering at a leading ISV, talked about how everyone owns quality now, in his team. Changes such as these are often large enough that they have a huge impact on organization structuring, individual careers, and the overall quality and acceptance of the product in the marketplace. This is exactly what we will see over the course of this book: to understand how software testing looked, what it is today, and what is expected to shape in the coming years.

Do We Still Need a Software Development Life Cycle?

Software development has come a long way. The processes, methods, technologies, and models have all changed over the years to align with the need of today. The software team has certainly become increasingly self-managing, thanks to the agile practices they have been exposed to in the last several years. They understand the importance and relevance of fast time to market, competition, and user feedback besides the core focus of product development and delivery. Given these positive changes that have set in, the question is, "Do we still need a software development life cycle (SDLC)?" Does it not add extra weight into the overall software implementation, making the overall approach more rigid and inflexible? What is the true value an SDLC brings to the table and is it justified to continue to use one or more of these models in the coming years? This is an important question to answer upfront, to understand how software testing will look like, and what testers will take on in the future.

At the core, an SDLC is a process to plan, build, engineer, test, and release a software system. This process helps teams enforce several important traits that are invaluable to the success of the project. To this extent, the model becomes a framework in real time to support end-to-end project execution. This includes the following:

Meeting and beating deadlines: An SDLC imbibes the sense of time in the team. The team is able to appreciate the need to meet and beat deadlines, track red flags, and bring in corrective course of action, when they have a certain model to follow.

Enhancing team productivity: SDLC model promotes knowledge and resource sharing, which is a great way to enhance a team's productivity. While individual team members are capable of their own research to explore ways to improve their productivity, an SDLC model instills better sense of collaboration and cross sharing, which greatly improves team's hands on productivity.

Establishing long-term vision: Without an SDLC, teams, although focused on the current development, often fail to have a vision into the future. An SDLC, as a model-based approach, forces them to think what is next for the next several releases, thus giving them an overall perspective into the future and long-term vision.

Enforcing adherence to a certain code of discipline: An SDLC brings formality to the team's operations. The onus is on the implementing team to either leverage this formality to bog down the team with mundane bureaucracies or use it to give the required structure to the effort, to bring in a positive discipline to encourage the team to deliver. When used well, the discipline and structure the SDLC brings in can further bond the team well, hence empowering them to work toward a common goal.

Balancing project constraints: Every project, however well funded it may be, faces constraints around time, cost, and quality.

It has to balance these out over the course of the project execution to ensure they are in control and positively impact the delivery of the project. In the absence of an SDLC, these constraints are more likely to get skewed making the effort very chaotic—all of these only add to the likelihood of the project to fail.

Having discussed the need of an SDLC, it is important to acknowledge that organizations are slowly and steadily moving away from a rigid single SDLC model execution. Hybrid style of operations where they adopt more than one model depending on the project they work on is gaining prominence. As long as organizations understand where the development landscape is heading, what project they are working on and what model to implement, and the flexibility and structure the SDLC offers despite its innate rigidity, they will already be half set for a successful implementation.

Did You Know?

1. Agile succeeds three times more often than waterfall[2] (Figure 1.3).
2. Software maintenance costs between 40% and 90% of overall project costs.[3]
3. Search content is available in 35 non-English languages in Google.[4] This is only continuing to grow showing the scale of global product development today.

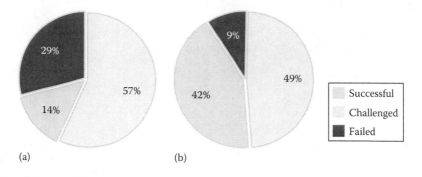

(a)   (b)

Figure 1.3 (a) Waterfall versus (b) agile implementation success rates. (From The CHAOS Manifesto, The Standish Group, https://www.mountaingoatsoftware.com/blog/agile-succeeds-three-times-more-often-than-waterfall, 2012.)

References

1. http://www.goodreads.com/quotes/tag/dynamism.
2. Cohn, M. https://www.mountaingoatsoftware.com/blog/agile-succeeds-three-times-more-often-than-waterfall.
3. iMasters Expert. 2014. http://imasters.expert/15-facts-programming-probably-know/.
4. Basu, S. 2010. http://www.makeuseof.com/tag/20-strange-interesting-facts-microsoft-google-apple/.
5. Kelly, H. 2015. Meet Google Alphabet—Google's new parent company. http://money.cnn.com/2015/08/10/technology/alphabet-google/index.html?iid=EL.

2

INFLUENCING A CHANGE
IN SOFTWARE TESTING

Change is the law of life. And those who look only to the past or present are certain to miss the future.

—**John F. Kennedy**[1]

This quote not just applies to individuals but also equally applies to teams, groups, organizations, and nations to ensure there is ongoing progress and evolution. Change is universal—it stretches its bounds beyond the span of time and discipline, and if there is one thing constant, it is the change itself.

What is change? In very simple terms, "it is to do something differently, start something new, or stop doing something that has already been in action." We often only associate change to a difference in what has been happening, but it can also include starting something afresh or bringing an action to an end. Essentially, any alternation to the current course of action can be looked at as a change.

Why Change Is Inevitable

We all appreciate certainty. Certainty gives a level of comfort. Steady state in operations is what we all strive for. If so, why is change inevitable? What would happen if we do not embrace change? Can this steady state not go on forever or at least for the foreseeable future? These reasons, discussed in the following, apply not just to software testing—these are relevant across all disciplines.

Change Drives Innovation and Innovation
Is Important to Both Survive and Thrive

Change and innovation go hand in hand. They are so tightly coupled that one is needed for another. Innovation is the process of change to bring in more efficiencies and productivity in what we do. While we often think innovation is important to thrive and stand out from the rest, it is sometimes important to even stay afloat in one's business. Figure 2.1 clearly shows the quadrants of innovation and how, depending on which quadrant you are in, the trait you emulate varies—be it agility, creativity, resilience, or versatility. Herein, the least ideal quadrant for anyone to be in is the recovery circumstantial stage, where you have to show resilience to pull yourself out of danger. The most ideal situation to be in is the competitive visionary state.

If we take the case of Apple as to the concepts given earlier, we all know how troubled an organization it was, a couple of decades back. With a much needed funding from its competitor Microsoft, it pushed itself from the "recovery circumstantial" state to "recovery visionary" state. It was a visionary back then, as it did not have any competition in the field of music players and mobile computing. It was versatile, showed creativity, and quickly jumped to the "competitive visionary" state that it is today, establishing itself as a clear leader in the mobile market.

The story to success of Minnesota Mining and Manufacturing Company (3M) was slightly different. It was completely in a different

Why innovate?

	Circumstantial	Visionary
Competition	*Agility* Achieve parity (acquire options)	*Creativity* Invent future (change playing field)
Recovery	*Resilience* Escape danger (repair damage)	*Versatility* Revitalize (regrow or reposition)

Figure 2.1   The need to innovate.

business—a business of manufacturing and mining, where it was facing severe losses. To pull itself out of danger, it chose an established business in the world of stationery supplies and thus moved itself from "recovery circumstantial" to "competitive circumstantial." From there, it established itself as a leader showing agility and creativity moving into the "competitive visionary" state with a number of out of box stationery supplies. For all of this innovation, a change was essential. The change helped organizations both survive and down the line thrive.

Change Breaks Monotony

When we repeat the same task we have been doing over time, boredom sets in. Boredom can bring down a person's efficiency and shut doors to one's creativity. Forcing a change in such situations helps break monotony and reinstate an excitement in what we do.

Change Breaks Fat, Dumb, and Happy (FDH) Syndrome

When people or organizations reach steady state and get too comfortable with it, they often get into a syndrome called FDH. This is especially true in large organizations, where employees get into a state of dismissal and are happy with the circle they have built around themselves. They do not want to do anything new and challenging, making it detrimental to both their and the organization's growth. This syndrome can push even a healthy organization into a troubled state, very soon. To ensure this syndrome does not set in or linger in for too long, change is inevitable.

Change Is Driven by External Factors

Change can be triggered by internal or external factors as shown in Figure 2.2. While an organization, as well as an individual, needs to constantly reevaluate internally to bring in the required changes, a number of external factors can bring in a sweeping change at hardly any notice. These may not even be in one's control, but the overall awareness that external factors can bring in the change and how to quickly respond to such changes will empower them to better embrace

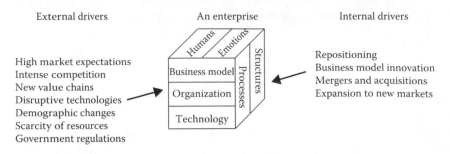

Figure 2.2 Drivers of change. (From https://www.business-prototyping.com/the-business-prototyping-manifesto/why-change-is-inevitable-but-progress-is-not/.)

the change. This is precisely the agile methodology's philosophy as well, to help organizations quickly adapt to external changes.

Change Is Normal

While the factors mentioned earlier drive a change, one should remember that the trigger need not be anything drastic. Change is often just part of the normal ongoing routine, to bring in continuous improvement. For example, one day, I could work from my office space, and on another day, I could decide I spend a few extra hours in a conference room, as that gives me more silence and better focus at my task. This is a very simple example of change in the normal setting. And oftentimes, the results from even such small changes could be phenomenal.

If we are able to acknowledge the basic fact that change is inevitable, we are able to better prepare ourselves for any oncoming change with a greater chance of reaping positive results from the whole exercise. But despite all of this understanding, teams continue to resist change. Why is that?

Resistance to Change

Oftentimes, although people and organizations fully comprehend the need for change and that it is inevitable, the pushback in embracing the change is high. There are a number of reasons why this resistance is shown—some of them are genuine reasons, while some are more of myths. Whatever the case may be, understanding the reasons and managing them to help the team align with the changes, even if not completely, at least to a large extent, is very important to reap a positive outcome. When this does not happen, there is more chaos than clarity, which can adversely impact the position of the team, from before the change. So understanding the reasons for resistance is an important area to be closely monitored.

Sense of Insecurity

Anytime a change is initiated, it is a deviation from the normal routine. Such deviation brings in a sense of insecurity and a host of open questions, which if unanswered further strengthens the insecure ground. Insecurity could be around one's own job, the group or organization's positioning, and competitive stand, among several others.

Lack of Trust

Even if the change is well planned and timed, there could be a general lack of trust in what the management conveys to the organization or what a manager conveys to his/her team members. This is not triggered by just that one change but is a belief and level of trust in the overall system. Trust has to be built and maintained at all times to ensure, when changes (of whatever magnitude) come in, resistance is manageable.

Lack of Visibility into What Is Coming

Tied into insecurity, the resistance is often triggered by the lack of transparency and view into what is coming in the future. In some cases, the management may have data on this but may not want to divulge details as yet. In other cases, the overall visibility may be lacking and the team will have to take in scenarios as the landscape unfolds. All of these lead to a fear of the unknown, forcing the thought process of whether a change is really required.

Comfortable with Status Quo

Oftentimes, organizations and individuals get very comfortable with the status quo that they do not want to change. Forcing in a change at regular intervals is a good exercise to ensure the team does not get too comfortable with the present and are nimble to take in a change when it comes in.

Fear of Failure

Even if there is belief in the change that is coming in, a change always brings in unsettled waters at least in the initial stages. With any such unsettlement, there is a fear of failure. What if the change brings in new uncertainties? What if I don't succeed? What if this leads to additional work? All of these questions and fears, especially of failing in the new ground, are strong reasons people resist a change.

Manner in Communicating the Change

While the change itself may be seen in positive light and people understand that it is for the good, oftentimes their acceptance to it is low, due to the way in which it is communicated to the target audience. It could be poorly timed, inadequately explained, discussed in a wrong medium (e.g., no in person meetings to explain the change and its impact), etc. In all of these, the resistance stems from the communication strategy adopted in conveying the change. Although this seems easily fixable, the damage it can cause when not done right the first time around can be huge.

Managing and Succeeding in Implementing a Change

Given the push back that often comes along with a change, managing a change through its life cycle is very important. When I say life cycle, a change has its own sequence of steps to follow right from planning for the change, breaking it down into phases, trying out the change in a small scale, expanding the scope of change, measuring the outcome of the change, and finally tracking it to closure. Change management is a process of its own to ensure the chances of succeeding through the change are enhanced. Through the course of handling the change process, here are some tips for enhancing the overall success:

Do the Required Homework

First, the stakeholders involved in a change must be convinced about the need to change. This involves a lot of homework: taking into account internal and external variables; evaluating the impact of the change (both positive and negative) and its toll on the team morale; timing the change; accounting for people at various levels, etc. All of these require a lot of homework depending on the scale of the change.

Maintain Required Levels of Transparency

As we have discussed in the earlier section, people often resist change as they do not get a full handle on what is going on. If the stakeholders involved in the change, take the effort to bring in the possible level of transparency it not only smoothens the process of accepting the change among entities involved but also enhances the overall chances of success.

Communicate Frequently

Communicating a change does not end up front. It is an ongoing communication process, where the stakeholders need to be in regular touch with entities to help them accept the change. Herein, the communication is not limited to just one-sided flow of information. They need to take the time to listen to the entities involved, hear out their concerns, and partake in resolving them to help implement the change.

Show Commitment in Making the Change a Success

By doing the preceding tips, the stakeholders are showing that they are committed to help the team succeed in not just implementing the change, but also enabling the change bring in positive difference in what they do. Such commitment from top down goes a long way in building trust beyond the scope of the current change.

Empower People Involved in the Change to Succeed

Communicating and being in touch is one side of the change management story. The more important side is to empower the team to succeed. This includes enabling them with the right resources, training, additional manpower, tools, etc., to support them in implementing the change.

When all of these tips are taken into account, change management not only turns out to be successful but also ironically can be a great team bonding and collaboration exercise along with simultaneously, bringing out the desired outcome from the change itself.

Software Testing Is Changing Too

Enough talked about change and change management, let's now get into the specifics of software testing. Software quality assurance and testing is changing, too. It has undergone a lot of changes in the last few decades, more rapidly in the last decade, and is already looking at more changes to come, in the next several years. Let's understand what is happening in this space including what are the variables that influence a change and what kind of changes they entail.

As we have seen in the earlier chapter, software testing has evolved and come a long way over the last few decades. From the days, where testing was done by the developer himself, to the current day, where the tester collaborates with the developer empowering him take on specific tasks, while elevating himself to do more user-centric quality work, we have come almost a full circle. However, James Bach talks of an interesting example, where when the tester's role changes and he is given a lot of freedom to figure out how to achieve product quality, it can be disorienting to start with. He compares this with a prisoner, who, when the prison cell is opened, complains of the cold air gushing in as opposed to the freedom that is now entailed on him.[3] All of this change is triggered by specific change agents. What are such change agents and what kind of changes do they bring into software testing? We will discuss the change agents under three groups—test methods, test attributes, and technology. Each of these is core and a part of the larger software testing umbrella itself and has continued to shape software testing as time changes. Let's understand them in greater detail as follows:

Software Development Methodologies

Practices adopted in any discipline form the core in defining the rigor of the operations taken up. Software development methodologies have by far been the most important change agent in how software testing has changed. These methodologies have laid foundations to determining when to test, how to test, and how much to test. They have had such a profound influence on testing to the extent of even shaping the state and recognition of software testing as an industry. In the waterfall days, for instance, testing has had a more gated approach. Testers were brought in toward the end of the release cycle, and their work was more rudimentary than being able to truly drive quality into the product. They were largely responsible for bringing in quality control, and if any issues were found later in the game, they were quite helpless, as most often they could not be fixed in the remaining amount of time. All of this had an abrupt stop and change when agile style of development came in, thus leaving the testers puzzled (as much as it did for the others on the product development team) on how to adopt agile practices. Testers were asked to go easy on test documentation, get involved from the early stages of development, build programming knowledge, and take on paired and test-driven development (TDD); while all of these were important to bring in more agility with a focus on end users, the change was too sudden and too drastic for testers to take in. The impact was so huge that it even pushed some back to the waterfall mode. This situation is now slowly stabilizing with a hybrid development approach coming in where teams are able to arrive at a customized agile approach, which takes in the core principles of agility, but offers the teams a fair amount of flexibility in their operations—they are now able to decide based on their past experience, own market, user base, and product as to how much of the test documentation is needed; what kind and percent of test automation makes sense, where TDD is their cup of tea; what is a tester's role in the continuous integration and development; and how can they empower the rest of the team, also own and appreciate quality, etc. Anytime a development methodology changes, the way software testing is done will also change. And when that change happens at an industry level (like in the days when agile came in), the change in software testing tends to be huge. The influence of software development methodology on testing is so high that even when this undergoes a small change within a given organization or project, the testing life cycle is impacted either directly or indirectly.

Testing Attributes

A test effort brings together several testing attributes. This includes functionality, UI, usability, performance, security, accessibility, and localization to name the core ones. All of these together determine the quality of the product to be released in the market. These attributes have themselves undergone a lot of changes owing to reasons such as market conditions, prevailing external forces, and end-user requirements, which have brought out significant changes in how, when, and how much of testing is needed. To that extent, this change agent can be called an agent and a change in itself. For example, as always, functionality continues to remain the key in determining the success of a product. But these other testing attributes are also gaining prominence, thereby determining what kind of testing is required and what together should constitute a test strategy. Let us take the case of security testing—during the days of desktop applications—security was not too much of an issue. It was more confined to physical application access or information exchange over a client–server model. A simple threat model and STRIDE analysis could easily take care of the security testing effort. But today, with the growth in online services, cyber security is a huge issue. Ethical hacking, penetration testing, tools to constantly monitor applications, and a checklist of vulnerabilities to track have all become critical. With all of this change, security testing has come into the limelight with a need for specialists and subject matter experts that need to be at least readily available for the test effort on demand, if not resident on the team. In one sense, I look at test attributes as a secondary change agent, as these are not changes that impact the testing effort directly. We will discuss the attributes and how they have changed in greater detail when we get to Chapter 4 to talk about the current state of the testing industry.

Technology

This is another huge change agent that has brought about changes in what we test and how we test. The technology world has itself undergone a rampant change in the last two decades, whether it be the Internet revolution at the very core or the newer computing technologies around cloud, social, mobile, analytics, wearable, augmented, and so on. Each of these has had a profound impact on the market at large and at a software development industry level. And the nice thing is that the industry is also aligning toward integrating these technologies—for example, the emergence of SMAC to bring together the social, mobile, analytics, and cloud computing worlds. Changes such as complexity of IT systems, fast adoption across markets, and how diverse systems are embracing varied technologies into their fold have all, in their own ways, brought in newer approaches and requirements to software testing. Technology is one area that continues to have a two-sided impact in software testing—both including how to test for the technology and how to leverage the technology in testing. Let's take cloud computing as an example here. With the introduction of the cloud when several applications are becoming online services, testers had to quickly gear up to test for *software as a service* and at the same time also leverage the cloud to build their test machines. *Infrastructure as a service* was a huge boon to testers that significantly saved their time with machine setup especially in areas such as performance testing. Oftentimes, we as testers are only heavily focused on how to test a technology, but to make ourselves more efficient and productive, now is the time for us to also see how to leverage the technology to make our lives simpler. The examples here are countless. If we start looking at all technologies from this two-pronged approach, it will bring in greater efficiencies in our scope of operations.

Market and End-User Requirements

This is yet another important variable that has brought in sweeping changes in what we test and how we test. We continue to be end-user representatives in the product team. The changing market requirements, whether it be the fast time to market, expectations for a rich feature set, or quick response to end-user wants, have all made test teams increasingly agile and nimble. It is still an open question whether agile development brought in these changes in the market or the market needs to bring in an agile style of development. Regardless, the dynamic testers have changed for the good, where they are able to respond to change requests very quickly. Also, they now understand that although there is a test complete before every product release, the test effort is truly ongoing, with constant interaction with end users even after live deployment. Also given how global software development has gotten to be, the reverse, where end users become testers, is also now a reality. They come in to evaluate the product and provide feedback before its release in the form of crowd-sourced testing. These have become valuable techniques to help with a quality release given the limited time and money on hand, despite the ever-increasing test scope.

Service-Oriented Mind-Set

This change agent ties back to the advent of cloud computing, where the overall industry mind-set changed into building service-oriented applications. Office, a very successful boxed product that is a cash cow for Microsoft now, has its online subscription model, Office 365. All products have moved into an online services model, which makes it easy and lightweight for users to leverage and, at the same time, provides full control and management power for the ISV in connecting with end users. This service-oriented style of development brings in newer requirements in testing around performance, security, and usability of the application, making these equally important as that of the core product functionality.

Markets and Compliances

With how complex the online market has gotten to be, it is becoming increasingly important to bring in checks and balances through compliances that systems have to adhere to and get certified on. For example, the U.S. government is slowly starting to mandate Section 508 to ensure systems are accessible. This calls for a rigorous round of testing, based on checklists such as Voluntary Product Accessibility Template that testers can leverage on top of their exploratory and scripted tests. Compliances in varied disciplines such as banking and health care have also brought in newer changes and opportunities to software testers.

While there are more such agents that bring in changes in software testing, these are core for us to track on an ongoing basis, as these together influence most of what happens in the software quality and testing world.

Another lingering question that people have, not specific to software testing, is how frequent should there be a change. This is not a very easy question to answer as most often all changes are not controlled internally. Several changes are driven by external factors where the organization or the team has no option but to change. In such cases, obviously one has to be ready to jump in and embrace the change as quick as possible with the least amount of impact. But for the others, which are internal planned changes or external changes that one can decide on and adopt, a certain amount of advance planning will really help. Also, giving a reasonable amount of time gap between two changes will not only give the teams a better opportunity to accept them but will also do justice to the existing process to stabilize, given the amount of time and money investment that would have gone into such an implementation.

From this point on, moving to Chapter 3, we will start looking at software testing in full detail, along with examples and case studies to see what kind of changes have taken place, where are we heading into the coming years, and whether we as a fraternity are ready for it.

Did You Know?

1. Google sets aside 20% of every employee's time for innovation.
2. The Sticky Notes from 3M that we all know was an idea of a 3M employee in the time that was set aside for employee innovation.
3. Studies show that Microsoft changed the world more than Apple did, as it was the first real software company.[4]
4. While we talk about varied change agents in the software industry, Steve Jobs as an individual is seen as a significant individual change agent that brought a huge change in the global software market.[5,6]

References

1. http://www.brainyquote.com/quotes/topics/topic_change.html.
2. https://www.business-prototyping.com/the-business-prototyping-manifesto/why-change-is-inevitable-but-progress-is-not/.
3. Heusser, M. 2013. http://www.cio.com/article/2387628/agile-development/how-to-adjust-to-the-changing-face-of-software-testing.html.
4. Glory, P.-E. http://www.businessinsider.com/yes-microsoft-did-change-the-world-more-than-apple-2011-9?IR=T.
5. Goldman, D. 2015. http://money.cnn.com/2015/05/17/technology/tim-cook-gwu-graduation/.
6. Baer, D. 2015. http://www.businessinsider.in/Steve-Jobs-said-his-life-changed-after-realizing-that-anyone-can-potentially-change-the-world/articleshow/46520103.cms.

3

WHAT DID WE DO SO FAR IN SOFTWARE TESTING?

I always knew looking back on my tears would bring me laughter, but I never knew looking back on my laughter would make me cry.

—**Cat Stevens**[1]

Oftentimes, we hear people saying there is no point looking back at the past and that one should just focus on the present and look into the future. I strongly believe in the need to look back. As the above quote rightly says, there are a lot of pluses and minuses that we can learn from, when we objectively set to analyze the past. Take, for instance, a retrospective meeting that is done at the end of a release. If looking back at the past is of no value, why do organizations place such emphasis on understanding the past and attempt to learn from them? The past has a lot of offer in terms of what went well and what could have been done better and often becomes a gauge to determine the next steps including key result areas. Software testing has undergone a lot of change in these past two decades. Testing practices, applications, tools, and technologies have all changed, and we looked at what some of those change agents were in the previous chapter. In this chapter we will primarily look at how we have been testing software applications in the past years. For the sake of this discussion, I will divide time frames into the past, present, and future, with **past being a time frame of until 2010, present being a time frame of until about 2016,** and **the future looking beyond that**. Such a timeline view will give us a logical understanding of not just the testing world in these times but also how the testing fraternity is aligning with the changing requirements in the software world and where in the Software Development Life Cycle (SDLC) testing had a place in. We will also look at what the Software Testing Life Cycle (STLC)

27

looked like, how various testing attributes were tested for, what did we learn from such practices which we can take forward, what from the past does not make sense now, and what kinds of testing metrics were used, to get an end-to-end view of testing in the yesteryears.

How Did Testing Fit into the SDLC of the Past Years?

Waterfall was the dominant SDLC model adopted in the past few decades. While other models such as the v-shaped and spiral were also in common use, waterfall had a dominant share in the market. A study conducted even as of 2010 showed that while organizations were increasingly moving on to using agile, about **59% mentioned they still use a combination of agile and waterfall methodology, 12% used purely waterfall, and 5% used purely agile**. Waterfall has been so deep rooted into the software development community at large, since the days of early product development that its reign has been very strong even just a few years ago.

And if we take in the pure waterfall model, the development phases have been very distinct and gated. Each phase has had ample time to get the required tasks in its scope of operations done—whether it be the initial stages of requirements gathering and design or the final stages of testing, deployment and release, and maintenance. The last few stages were often feared to be more time constrained, but in the traditional waterfall days, where products were more boxed in nature with long release cycles often running into months, this was not too much of a concern. Testers often did not have any communication with the rest of the development team until their work started later in the game. This was one of the huge downsides of the waterfall model where teams worked in a very disconnected manner. They lacked the larger contextual understanding of their role and their tasks, leading to a very loosely coupled effort that ended up impacting end-user satisfaction. Even if a formal project management effort tied up all these loose ends, there was a lot of drain in terms of overall development costs, cost of quality with quite a gap to be fixed, between end-user requirements and the delivered product. While this style of development has not gone away completely today, a large portion of it has been washed away with the increasing adoption of the agile style of development.

How Did the STLC Itself Look?

The STLC has had its independent flow both in the days of the water-fall and agile. The rigor with which it has been implemented and the customized flows it has had have undergone change, but at a high level, having an STLC has been greatly valuable to bring in a desired level of discipline in the overall testing effort. The varied efforts traditionally adopted in a software test life cycle include test strategy creation, test plan creation, test design, test execution, defect management (including regression testing), and test sign-off. Test teams have also engaged in not just testing on non-live environments but also in debugging, track-ing, and testing issues in the live environments. Testers continue to be end-user representatives on the team but how they have contributed in being such end-user representatives has varied over the years. During the yesteryears that we are talking about, even though they represented the end user's quality needs, they were not empowered to do much, given how late in the game they got into the testing cycle. Even if they had great ideas and suggestions, they were not very empowered to influencing them from being implemented. Before we discussed each of the stages of the testing life cycle in greater detail, let's talk about the salient features that characterized a test effort in the past:

1. Heavy emphasis on test document and test artifact creation
2. Strong focus on black box testing, even if the test effort itself was independent in nature
3. Gated approach to start the test execution effort only after coding was complete
4. Heavy reliance on metrics that often don't convey the true meaning of quality
5. Onus of complete quality passed on to testers, with a lack of accountability among the rest of the product team
6. Main focus on product functionality, with nonfunctional areas such as performance, security, usability, and accessibil-ity often taking a complete back seat
7. Pressure to sign off on the test effort to release on time, despite having started late

All of these core characteristics made it very difficult to deliver quality releases. The tester was also demotivated as his efforts seemed to go unnoticed. If at all any, he was only made visible when there were live issues seen in the production environment. He did not have an environment to thrive and was merely surviving which made it difficult for him to collaborate with the rest of the product team. He was seen a step down compared to his counterparts in the design and development teams. All of these did not offer a very conducive environment both to the quality of the product and to the morale in the team. While all of these sound not so positive, the activities in the STLC were themselves of great value when seen individually and implemented at the right levels. So, what are those activities and what is done when each of them is taken up. Let's herein talk about these activities one by one.

Test Strategy

When a test effort was initially conceptualized as an independent activity to be performed by testers who were not involved in the development effort, the need for a test strategy came in. This is a document that talks about the product, its architecture, what are the varied test areas (for which test plans would subsequently be created), entry and exit criteria for the overall release, resource mapping identifying testers who would be working on varied components, what the group's overall test and defect management practices would be, etc. This has served as a very valuable document in the waterfall days, helping the testers pause and understand the larger context of what they were involved in, how each other's work interlaced, what are some of the common practices in the team, etc. However, it does take time to create a test strategy. In a large group where a number of modules are being tested, creating a test strategy can even turn out to be a one-month exercise. This is a lot of time, to be spent upfront, but if the right efforts are made into shaping the strategy into relevant and meaningful pieces of information for the group, it can pay off in the long run. For it to continue to be of value to the team, it is important for the test strategy to be maintained and updated regularly as well as used by the team as and when required.

Test Planning

Some teams combine the test strategy and the test plan to save time involved in creating them as well as the overhead of maintaining multiple documents, but in the truest essence of the traditional testing life cycle, these were both independent documents. After creating a test strategy, a small group of testers would be tasked with creating individual module level test plans. Let's say a test plan to test the web workflow, a test plan for the desktop version, a test plan for the reporting module, a test plan for the overall database implementation, one from the performance and load angle, one for security of the application, and so on. This assigned individual responsibilities enabling a small group of testers to focus in detail on their specific areas, define scenarios, what kinds of tests they plan to take on, what test environment is needed, what are the test estimates, risks and mitigations, and so on. Such plans gave the tester the time to think through all elements of testing upfront, even before the testing could commence. Test plans again brought in their own value despite the time and effort involved upfront, but as mentioned given these overheads, teams soon moved into combining the strategy and the plan such that everyone would use the core common principles but individual customized test scenarios.

Test Design

A lot of emphasis was placed on designing test cases. While some teams left test cases at scenarios level, most teams would take in the scenarios from the test plans to elaborate them into a set of individual test cases of varying levels of detail. Some test cases were so detailed that a new tester coming into the test effort can merely review the test cases to understand application workflows. While such granularity helped ensure no confusion on what tests were executed and also to train new people, it also meant that so much more time was being spent on writing test cases, during which the tester could have actually tested the product. Maintenance was also a huge overhead where even for a small feature change, the tester had to spend a lot of time updating the test cases.

Test Execution

By the time the tester gets his hands dirty into the actual test execution effort, often much time would have elapsed in getting the test planning done and the artifacts created. By this time, the rest of the product team would have most likely gotten into the product release mind-set. The testers were highly focused on executing the scripted test cases that they had earlier designed. We will discuss what kinds of testing they took on, in a subsequent section, but the discussion around tester's productivity would often linger around how many test cases were executed. This was considered very important because the testers had to sometimes achieve unrealistic numbers to the tune of even 250 test cases a day. This made execution a very monotonous activity hindering the true creativity of a tester. A tester's typical day also involved recording results from all these executed tests and also filing defects for issues found. All of this added to the tester's documentation overhead where he was often very exhausted at the end of the day, not leaving any room for the tester to try exploratory tasks.

Defect Management

A lot of emphasis was rightly placed on defect management. The tester was responsible all the way from finding the defect, to filing it, to following up to getting it fixed, regressing it in the right environment, adding new test cases that map to the defect, and updating the regression suite, to ensure the new test cases are taken into account in subsequent milestones. While each of these activities is very important on their own, the larger question was whether the tester was truly empowered to drive defects to closure. They often had no say or did not participate in defect triages giving supreme powers to the developer to fix defects they see fit. The tester who had the true understanding of what impact the defect had on end users did not often have an opportunity to raise them in the defect triage meetings. Defect management was also in most cases a laborious process with room for quite some efficiency gains, as the testers and developer's machine environments did not align. These were the days cloud computing technologies were not very prevalent or were just coming into mainstream market, necessitating a lot of time to be spent on setting up the test environment. There were a lot of wasted cycles around trying to reproduce issues and help the developer get on to the same page with that of the tester in understanding the issue fully, regardless of how detailed the defect report was. All of this made defect management an overhead despite its importance and value.

Test Sign-Off

For the entire product team, this was the much awaited activity from a tester's side. The tester, after carefully weighing in all the outcomes of his test execution effort, results from defect management, regression suites, code coverage, and metrics that were defined for test exit in the test strategy, would be in a position to make the sign-off call. This was a call made by the test manager and director in consultation with individual test leads who represented specific test teams. Test sign-off was a very busy and important day, as the decision was a big one and also was so close to the release date that the anticipation would be very high. Early in the days, when metrics were not used as much, this call was a very subjective one to take, but over the course of the years, the test team implemented objective metrics that made the sign-off decision more easy to make and reliable to act upon.

Other Activities in Which Testers Were Involved

These were activities that not all testers did on all teams but were frequent enough that they are worth mentioning here.

Test Environment Setup   While in most cases build engineers helped with the test environment setup, since this was the age before cloud-based setup became popular, test setup was often a very laborious and time-consuming task. In the pre-cloud days, virtualization helped them quite a bit in setting up machine instances where testers needed cross-platform configurations across varied operating systems and browsers. Build engineers who were experts with machine setup often helped save a lot of cycles for testers, but such an external dependency and the wait for a testable build also meant that the tester's valuable test cycles were often eaten into.

Code Coverage Test Runs   This was one of those early techniques that testers used to bring in traceability and objectivity into the test efforts. Testing on instrumented builds, testers were able to show case, what code paths their test efforts covered, what were the dead code areas, if any, and plan for any additional testing that was needed. Code coverage run was often taken up after one full test pass was completed and most often after test automation was built. While code coverage runs can be taken up even on manual test efforts, testers often took them up on automated test suite runs. Code coverage results were also used to determine where to improve test automation coverage on, in the coming milestones. I've listed this under additional activity for testers, since code coverage runs were not always performed or even if they were done regularly, it was not always a task taken up by testers.

Static Code Reviews   As mentioned in the earlier chapter, testing initially started off as an activity taken up by the developers themselves. Later, when independent testing came into the picture, testers were an entity of their own on the team, but their focus was heavy on the black box side. Even automation did not stretch into the internal architecture of the application much, but rather focused on the top layer functional automation and UI automation. However, in some teams, testers were involved in reviewing the code written by the developers at a static (nonexecution level). These were testers who understood code, who had the knowledge of programming languages, and who were able to stretch themselves into these extended horizons of testing. Such activities certainly helped them bond better with the rest of the product team and also empowered them understand the nuances of the application implementation better than the ones who merely focused on black box testing. The debate on whether testers should know programming languages continues to this day. There continue to be excellent black box functional testers who know nothing about programming languages but who can find some top-notch bugs in the application and think exceedingly well from an end user's shoes. That said, the additional value brought in by testers who do static code reviews cannot be discounted.

Live Site Debugging   In the waterfall days, especially during the early stages of product release, quick fix engineering was a common phenomenon. These were quick releases also called hotfixes to patch issues found in the live environment and most often reported by the end users or people using the product on the field. Since these were user facing issues, teams had very little time to debug, fix, test, and rerelease the product. Testers played a very active role in shipping hotfixes to resolve such live issues.

How Test Attributes Were Tested

While the test attributes have largely remained the same over the years—be it functional, usability, performance, security, localization, etc.—the way we have tested them has changed significantly. In this section, let's briefly look at how we used to test for each of these attributes in the yesteryears.

Functionality

This was the prime focus in a testing effort. A large percent of test cases were focused on validating the functional aspects of the application. This would include the user facing functionalities, database, reporting and administrative level functionalities, and so on. Functional test cases formed a large portion of most test suites—be it the full test pass, sanity test pass, or regression test pass. Even for a build to be certified as test ready, the functional workflows would be the main elements to be tested. Application Programming Interfaces (APIs) and web services grew in importance over the years, but early in the years APIs were not very prevalent, thus focus on functional testing specific to APIs and web services were limited. Also most of the functional testing was done manually. Teams typically picked UI test cases for automation with limited number of functional tests that were built into the automation suite. As they started understanding the importance of Return on Investment (RoI) on test automation, an increasing focus on functional automation was brought in.

UI

User Interface elements that brought the overall application's design together were given a lot of importance in a testing effort. This was typically started a little later than the functional test cycle to allow room for the UI to stabilize. Positioning of page elements, color, font, style, and rendering were all taken into account in testing an application's UI. UI defects were one of the high bug count categories among the overall set of defects a tester reported.

Usability and Accessibility

While usability and accessibility were not new areas of testing back in the day, not much emphasis was given to these areas. The product team at large was more focused on functionality and UI and believed that these two together would garner enough customer satisfaction. These elements started gaining more visibility, when the market was open for more players to come in. As competition came in, these became differentiating factors helping one stand out against another. There was an increased appreciation for usability, especially around areas of simple application usage, intuitive workflows, graceful error scenarios, etc., all of which hoping to earn better customer acceptance in the marketplace. Around the same time, accessibility standards such as Sec 508, DDA, and WCAG all started entering mainstream industry practices, building a niche need for accessibility testing to accommodate application usage for the disabled.

Performance

Load, stress, overhaul, and capacity planning have all been important elements in software implementation and testing since the early years, but again, they had a back seat. Companies were not so bothered of their performance and aspects such as availability, page load, and response times. In my experience, this has also been primarily because of lack of competition. The large software players were monopolies who controlled the market. Even if their performance was not up to the mark, users had no choice but to stick with them. With all of this confidence that the large players had built over the years, performance testing was more of a routine check that was conducted as opposed to a real value add in the product. Performance testing was also done slightly later in the game, where even if issues were reported, they were not acted upon in the same milestone. Given the time and effort that goes into fixing them, they were often pushed out to be considered in subsequent milestones. Performance testers were slowly gaining prominence, but it was still largely about functional testing and test automation.

Security

Security has become a prime area of focus in recent years with growth in online presence and increased penetration of services in the IT industry. Back in the days of desktop applications, security was more of a physical than a digital concern. Security testing was done but was primarily limited to STRIDE—covering Spoofing, Tampering, Repudiation, Information Disclosure, Denial of Access, and Elevation of Privilege. It was largely related to authentication and authorization-related issues and was often covered with a simple threat model analysis that testers used as a base for their testing efforts. While teams understood the importance of security testing, this also took a back seat when compared to functional and UI testing efforts. Time permitting, teams conducted one to two rounds of security testing toward the end of the milestone. At an industry level, knowledge of both security attacks and testing techniques were fairly limited. However, over the years, security attacks have been increasingly complex and sophisticated, necessitating newer security testing tools and techniques. Guidelines from bodies such as Open Web Application Security Project have greatly helped testers gain understanding and bring in a focused security testing effort. Pen testing organizations have done exceedingly well in the closing years of this "past time frame" bringing in newer testing practices including ethical hacking to gear up the industry to handle security well.

Globalization

Globalization has always played an important role in a software development effort. While it was often delayed than a core English release, this has been a more mature testing practice even from the early years compared to areas such as performance and security. Product release in global markets, for instance, an operating system from Microsoft that was made available in several languages or, say, a software from

Adobe that went into global markets, was something that was fairly common. Core testers on the team took on internationalization and pseudo localization testing followed by localized testers who would come in for localization testing. In addition to localization testing, a team of linguistic experts would also come in to verify contextual product implementation and suggest changes, if any, to enhance product acceptance in local markets. While the process in itself was fairly mature, the challenge with globalization was that it was done too late in the game to incorporate the process tightly into the software testing and development life cycles.

Other Testing Types

Other than the core testing types or attributes discussed earlier, testing has always had more breadth to it. The fascinating aspect to software testing is that it is vast running both horizontally and vertically. Domains bring in a new dimension to software testing too where one could specialize in domain-specific areas such as testing for banking applications, health-care applications, etc., and building a niche around the workflows in each of them. Some of the additional testing types that have traditionally existed in the world of software testing include the following:

Test Automation   Automation in software testing is a very broad area. It continues to evolve on an ongoing basis and has been of significance since the early years. The ways in which automation is done, what kind of tools and frameworks are used, what is automated, and when and how it is done are the ones that undergo change over time. In the yesteryears, automation largely focused on the UI elements and some functional aspects. Record and play tools were the ones primarily used and most of these were commercial tools since open source was not very popular or mature back then. Automation was typically done after a few rounds of manual testing that ensured the system was stable and testers had a good knowledge of the application's workflows. Automation testers did not necessarily have a very good understanding of the system's internals and relied on record and play tools to capture the system's workflow in an automated manner. While this was quick and convenient to build on an automation suite, it had a lot of issues around reliability and stability of the code, especially when the UI underwent changes.

Compatibility Even back in the years, compatibility testing was of very high significance and value in a test effort. Tests would have to be run on varied operating systems and browsers to ensure they rendered fine and worked well. There were often defects that were specific to a given operating system and browser combination that had to be fixed and verified. A couple of unique characteristics about compatibility testing in the past are as follows:

- *Lack of adequate infrastructure to run compatibility tests*: It was about 2004–2005 when cloud-driven infrastructure came into place with its offerings around infrastructure as a service. A few years before then virtualization was in vogue where testers would set up virtualized machines to switch to and run their tests across varied operating systems and browsers. Until all of these came in, the task of machine set up for compatibility testing was quite tedious involving a plethora of physical machines. Besides operating systems and browsers, other applications traditionally taken into account in compatibility included antivirus software, application firmware, and printer and other device software, as these were often seen influencing factors that may interfere with the functionality of the application under test.
- *Need for optimization*: Although the testing matrix for compatibility was relatively smaller back in the days compared to what it is today, the need for optimization was felt back then as well, primarily due to lack of testing time and lack of the required infrastructure. Optimizations would be done based on market usage of varied operating systems and browsers based on which tests would be grouped into full test pass and sanity test pass suites to enhance test coverage within the constraints of time and cost.

Integration Often since several modules were being developed and tested as individual pieces, integration testing was very important back in the days. A tester would herein tie all the pieces together to ensure workflows worked well end to end. It was not until later in the game that the application would be ready to test end to end and while some automation was leveraged for this, integration tests were also largely done manually. Most often automation would begin after an integration test pass where testers were able to gauge the stability of the application.

Acceptance   This test pass often aligned with the exit criteria defined in a test strategy. This would include a suite of cases mostly end-user scenarios that would certify the readiness of the application for external consumption. The acceptance test pass would often also be mapped to metrics such as percent of test cases passed and percent of tests failed in the given priority category, all of which together would help the test manager make the call on the application's readiness for release.

Testing in the past, although later in the game, had its own rigor and discipline. It was a lengthy and elaborate process not all of which truly added value to the quality of product under test. We will discuss more of this around testing metrics, pros and cons of testing back in the days, in the subsequent sections.

Regression Testing   A suite of test cases that were built, maintained, and run by testers to ensure defect fixes or new check-ins did not break any existing implementation has been popular for over three decades now. Regression testing has been given the attention it deserved from the very beginning—the only difference being over the years the tools that have been used and the way tests were prioritized have changed. Early in the years all tests used to be run as part of the regression suite. Not much optimization was really done. Also most of these tests were run manually. Over the years, testers have started adopting smart regression testing strategies—this included identifying the right set of test cases that together gave the required level of coverage rather than executing all tests. Also critical tests from newer defects that were filed were added on to the regression test suite. Teams started understanding that the automation RoI from a regression test suite was much higher than in any other area and thus these were identified as good candidates for test automation. Despite all the evolution regression testing has been going through, it still was more of a downstream activity in the yesteryears that would happen after check-ins were made and builds came into the hands of the tester.

Testing Metrics

The concept of using metrics has always been practised in the world of software testing. Metrics have greatly helped bring in objectivity into a test effort, which can otherwise get subjective. Metrics were primarily used to understand the quality of the product and the productivity of a test effort—including the overall progress made and that of an individual tester. They were typically divided into two categories to fit into either quality metrics or test effort/management metrics:

- Test management metrics
  - Quality of testing
    - Number (#) of defects found in testing/(# of defects found in testing + # of acceptance defects found after release)
  - Test efficiency metrics
    - Metrics on test execution and pass percentages
  - Test phase metrics
    - # of bugs raised and closed per phase
  - Test coverage
    - # of test requirements versus # of total requirements
- Product quality metrics
  - Various views of defect metrics
    - Defects by resolution
    - Defects by injection phase
    - Defects by priority and severity
    - Defects by type
    - Defects by cause
    - Defect patterns

While several of these metrics are still valuable today, some of the metrics were turning out to be mundane driving additional unwanted overhead into a tester's daily routine. For example, the number of tests executed on a daily basis would often turn out to be a competition between testers to see who executed the most. Sometimes, these numbers were irrationally high to the extent of 250 test cases per tester per day, making it a huge compromise on the actual quality of the test effort. While it was good to see the use of metrics in the past years too, this was an area that needed a lot of improvement and customization to realize the true connect between these numbers and how they translated into an application's quality.

Case Studies from Our Past Years of Software Testing

Having talked about how testing was done in the past in detail, I thought it would be useful to include a couple of case studies from our experience at QA InfoTech. These are examples of projects that were implemented either in a waterfall model or a pseudo waterfall-agile model. These talk about what the project was, what were the requirements/challenges, and what solutions we proposed for the client to help alleviate the challenges, even if execution was in a pure waterfall model.

Case Study 1

Client Client was a leading publisher and aggregator providing educational content, tools, services, and other resources to academic libraries across the United States, Canada, and the rest of the world.

Problem QA was not involved rigorously in decision-making and requirement changes. This made it difficult to manage a well-balanced quality effort. Also there was no collective ownership for quality, making it difficult for test to own up the gaps in the effort of the rest of the product team as well.

Additional Challenges

- There were a lot of requirement documents and multiple versions of them to be reviewed and incorporated into the test effort.
- A lot of valuable time was lost in reviewing the requirement documents and exchanging comments.
- Multiple features and workflows were grouped in single documents, making it laborious for the QA team to track changes and maintain versions.

- The common repository was sometimes not updated with the latest versions of the documents, hence leaving the QA team clueless of what changes came in.
- Due to all of this documentation chaos, QA team ended up logging issues that were rejected—this was a blow not just on the overall quality effort additionally impacting testing costs and time, but it also impacted the morale of the team adversely.
- The test cases count ran into thousands, making it a herculean task to keep them updated per changes in the requirement documents.
- Test cases were maintained in excel sheets—multiple copies of such cases in circulation were getting impractical to manage.
- QA cycles were typically 8–10 days long.
- QA team executed all test cases in each and every cycle, with no optimization done.
- Production releases were scheduled quarterly—live issues were pending to be fixed for a very long time.
- There was a lot of dependency on the release engineering team for build deployments on QA environment.
- Most importantly, only QA was considered responsible for quality.

Solution   The QA team from QA InfoTech proposed a more collaborative approach that not only led to substantial time savings but also cut down on redundant efforts. All of the following suggestions below together enhanced the overall quality of the product.

Due to the onshore–offshore model, there were certain other communication challenges as well that needed to be addressed.

- QA team decided to have some overlapping time (2–3 hours daily) with the onsite team.
- QA team was made a part of all update meetings, making it a more participative environment—this led to other positive changes including more collaboration and a cooperative execution approach among team members.
- Since QA team also became a part of the change request process, any sort of confusions were avoided at the first place leading to a huge savings in time and effort.

- Effective version control using SourceForge was implemented leading to an 80% effort reduction.
- Since everyone had access to the latest versions, no unnecessary defects were logged—this significantly brought down the percent of invalid defects that were filed.

These provided a positive change to issues the team was facing and also opened doors for a more collaborative approach in owning quality collectively.

Case Study 2

This case study is an example of a project where we faced quite a few challenges owing to the waterfall style of operations and how we turned it around with a blend of agile that we brought in. Since agile was also a fairly common development methodology in that "past" time period we are talking about, I wanted to discuss this case study that runs from waterfall well into an agile implementation.

Client The client in discussion here is a leading education technology and services company for higher education and a global publisher of books in the United States. They have a presence across 1000 higher educational institutions in North America and are used by over two million students. They offer digital textbooks, instructor supplements, online reference databases, distance learning courses, test preparation materials, and materials for specific academic disciplines. With their expertise in student response system, they focus on formative assessment and pedagogy, making it a perfect audience response system for the growing number of K-12 customers to corporate training environments and tradeshows.

Challenges

- Test releases were quite late, averaging just 7–10 days before the target deliverable date.
- Test passes were long (in days) running well over 2–3 months.
- Engineer(s) work estimates were exceptionally inaccurate. For instance, a task estimated around 10 hours would often take around 20–25 hours to complete.

- Quality was not at desired levels—the bug counts soared with each release.
- Roles and responsibilities were not well defined—work on a particular task would completely stop if the person in charge was not available.
- QA/testers and developers rarely collaborated with each other.

Solution To address these challenges, we adopted an agile process on our project. This helped us save time and minimize queries and false failures. Our process included adopting the following:

- Sprint dashboard—a master list of all the functionality desired in the product
- Sprint sizing meeting—to describe, prioritize, and estimate features
- Daily Scrum—to involve all team members in daily status sync meetings
- Sprint review meeting—to discuss what has been accomplished during the sprint

Approach We at QA InfoTech worked on this process—agile methodology (Figure 3.1).

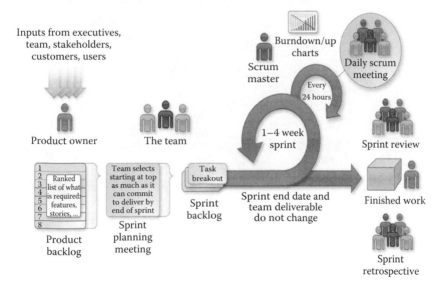

Figure 3.1 The Agile Scrum framework. (From http://agileforall.com/resources/introduction-to-agile/.)

Client Benefits

- All—Management, development, and QA teams started using the scrum dashboard regularly.
- All releases started falling into place in terms of time—We have not missed the target date in the past last 2½ years.
- Sprint/iteration timings became much shorter—Releases were scheduled every 4–5 weeks.
- Efforts became precise—Sometimes, we undersized the user story.
- New issues found in live environments came down significantly—By over 75% across all platforms, and continues to fall down with each release.
- Teams were more empowered to make decisions that will benefit the company or clients.
- Teamwork—Daily interaction with developers gave better insights into client wants and needs.

Analyzing the Past

Having looked at the process and methodology of software testing and quality assurance in the past, let's analyze to see what made sense and what was more of an overhead that did not really add much value:

- The past definitely brought in rigor and discipline to software testing. It helped define and implement the software testing life cycle.
- Given the detailed documentation that was in place, ramping up new testers into a given project or even to bootstrap them into the world of software testing was more feasible.
- It certainly gave a meaning and relevance to the world of independent software testing. Early in the days, the developers would themselves take on testing and this period was an important one to establish the need for independent testing.
- There was more reliability in certain efforts such as localization testing where efforts could commence after fully verifying the readiness of the product in core English.
- This was a time period where definitions and detailed processes were chalked out for several areas of testing—for example,

the threat modeling for security, base-lining and profiling for performance, and standards for accessibility. Similarly frameworks for automation started taking shape toward the end of this time frame.

On the flip side, there were lot of process inefficiencies in this time frame:

- A lot of emphasis was placed on documenting test efforts, scenarios, and creation of artifacts. To add to this, these artifacts were hardly used in the actual test effort. A test strategy was often turning into an obsolete piece of document that hardly anyone referred to. Sections such as resource allocation in the strategy did not bring in much relevance or use to anyone on the team.
- The cycle was such that testers hardly communicated with the rest of the product team. Or even if they did, it was hardly with the developers and build engineers bringing in a lot of disconnect in terms of interpersonal team collaboration as well as product understanding and updates.
- Testers were often not part of important activities such as triage meetings. This held them back from being the true voice of end users on the team. Even if they had useful information to convey about the user impact and quality of the product, they often did not have the right platform to convey it on.
- Focus was more on functional and UI elements of testing, while areas of specialization such as performance, security, and accessibility were not of significance early in the years.
- As product teams were moving waterfall to agile, not just development teams were impacted. Test teams also had a huge impact. In fact changes were more prominent on the test side of things—although these were positive changes, it look a lot of time to embrace them given the magnitude of changes involved.
- Testing metrics were not very realistic enough to promote healthy competition. Metrics such as number of tests executed per day were more detrimental to the tester morale than being of much relevance to understanding his progress and status.

- All of these made testing expensive and time consuming. This not only impacted the quality of the product and the positioning of the tester but also often led to questioning the value testing brought to the table.

Software Testing Career Options

This was also a period where software testers were not held very high in reputation. Testers often chose the profession without being able to land themselves in software development roles. Testers who often chose to take on manual testing were not very well respected for their contributions, and their inputs regarding the quality of the product were also taken in at face value. While it is not possible to generalize this at an industry level, this was the larger prevailing sentiment. However, this was also the time frame where career options were beginning to take shape. A tester could either progress in the individual technical charter of becoming a test analyst and architect or could take the managerial route to become a lead, manager, and director. Specialization roles also slowly started coming in around the end of this time period, where testers could become performance, automation, security, localization, and usability specialists. In all, although this time period was not a very glorious one for software testing, it was a very important one to set foundations around testing processes and careers.

In all this time period until 2010, although there were downsides to the overall testing discipline, strong roots were laid to establish independent software quality assurance. This was also the period where quality started moving from control to assurance. Thus, it laid the foundation for several new beginnings to further come in and set a strong example for adapting to newer changes that were on the horizon.

Did You Know?[2]

1. The most commonly adopted software testing techniques used today (coverage and black box) were developed in the 1960s and 1970s.

2. The cost to develop software is directly proportional to the cost of testing:
   a. Testing accounts for **50%** of all prerelease costs
   b. Testing accounts for **70%** of all postrelease costs
3. We often go after the "wrong bugs":
   a. 33% of all faults failed less than once in every 5000 execution years.
   b. 2% of all faults caused the common failures (more than once every 5 execution years).
4. Testing/debugging can worsen reliability:
   a. Each correction had a 15% chance of creating a problem as large as the problem it was supposedly fixing.

References

1. http://www.brainyquote.com/quotes/keywords/looking_back.html.
2. http://www2.informatik.hu-berlin.de/rok/zs/WS0506/data/slides/zs11_04SW-Testing(Guest_Lecture).pdf.
3. http://agileforall.com/resources/introduction-to-agile/.

4

TESTING IN THE
PRESENT TIMES

Planning is bringing the future into the present so that you can do
something about it now.

—**Alan Lakein**[1]

In line with this quote, we currently are seeing a very dynamic present. Things are evolving by the day in the technology space and the
ones that are able to maintain an edge for themselves are not the ones
that look just at the present but also plan for the future and incorporate them into the present. The present is always an exciting period of
time. It has a strong connection with the past where one applies learnings from previous experiences. It sets the base for the future with the
current planning that is taking up. In addition, it is the time for the
current set of activities rolling out. We will look at software testing in
the present in this chapter from a time period of around 2011 to about
2016. Besides the connection this period has with both the past and
the future, the present today is very important to understand exhaus-
tively. I say this because the entire software development industry is
going through a very interesting phase. Changes that are paradigm
and of large impact are occurring as we speak. These are redefining
the IT industry's positioning and penetration for the coming years
and what we see are certainly indicative of the present paving way for
a very exciting future.

Specifically to the world of software testing, what does this present
hold? How does the STLC look like in the larger SDLC umbrella,
what tasks are testers taking on today, what trends are we seeing
emerging, what has changed in comparison to the past, what to watch
out for as we move into the future, how is a tester's role changing,

and what metrics are we measuring today are some of the core points, among others, that we will discuss in this chapter.

What Has Changed in Today's Style of Development?

When we discussed the "past" in the previous chapter, we looked at how, at an industry level, we were moving from a waterfall to an agile model. This also included the phase where most organizations were aggressively pursuing agile in the supposedly truest form. This sudden jump from a traditionally adopted model to something completely new and drastically different has been quite an impact on product teams. As with any new model that evolves, the industry at large had a lot of issues understanding and implementing agile in the early years. However, around the start of the "current" time frame we are looking at, organizations started realizing the true requirements and goals of the agile manifesto and how they can be implemented as a customized version to meet their needs. Oftentimes this was even a pseudo agile model that had a slight flavor of other development life cycles as and when warranted. By the time teams settled in the agile model of development we are already into another flavor of development, which further empowers teams reap the benefits of what the agile world promises to offer—this is the world of DevOps—a world where agile has become even more lean in its operations and has become truly collaborative in bringing teams together. DevOps is a development model that seemingly includes only development and operations, but in its drive to promote continuous integration and delivery has a very important role for testers to play. Let's briefly look at how the DevOps model looks and what is a tester's role therein.

DevOps and Changing Role of Test in DevOps

In the earlier days, even with full-blown agile implementation, although test was involved earlier in the life cycle, there were dependencies that test had with other teams making the overall effort linear in some sense. For example, until something testable came in from development test teams were still not completely occupied. Development, test, and operations teams were still operating as individual units despite working in parallel. DevOps has changed this where all teams come together as a single unit to promote continuous delivery. In specific scenarios, DevOps is seen as an evolution over the agile model (that focuses on collaboration at the plan, code, build stages), continuous integration (that focuses on collaboration at the plan, code, build, test stages), and continuous delivery (that focuses on collaboration at the plan, code, build, test, release stages). DevOps is seen as a model that focuses on collaboration and value proposition at the plan, code, build, test, release, deploy, and operate stages). It is a model where continuous integration and delivery is made possible, and the entire team is able to operate collaboratively yet independently in product development.

One of the main requirements in a successful agile implementation is for a demonstrable software at the end of each release. While teams understood this requirement and had an agreed set of user stories developed and tested, the developed software was still not pushed to production due to several constraints and limitations on the operations side. Environment availability, configuration dependencies, and infrastructure support were some of the reasons, among others, that handcuffed the operations team in taking on their tasks to completion. And all of this was not purely an operations issue. Business readiness to launch including pricing models, competitive analysis, marketing readiness, and stakeholder sign-off all had to come together to make ongoing release to production a reality.

DevOps comes in with such a promise to look past the core development and test teams and enable the others on the product team as well join in to support anytime deployment. What this calls for is increasing levels of automation—traditionally we have looked at automation purely from a testing and testing coverage standpoints, whereas DevOps brings in a completely new definition, to automation. In today's scenario, automation is all about automating build deployments, test processes, unit tests and enhancing overall test coverage through code coverage, all with the goal of making the development process fast, hassle-free, reliable and code quality robust.

Unlike the agile model that came in all of a sudden, in a time when IT professionals were very deep rooted in their traditional styles of development, DevOps has been a more gradual shift. Since it also evolved from the agile model as a base, teams have been more comfortable adapting to the requirements of DevOps. Some of the core requirements that make DevOps feasible include a strong regression test suite, instrumented code, system configurability, back and forward code compatibility, and keeping track of overall product dependencies, among others.[2]

Granted DevOps is a robust model that is here to stay; how has it really impacted the software testing fraternity? The core principles of DevOps around continuous delivery and readiness to ship at short intervals and in parallel work among all teams are the ones that have been impacting the test discipline.

What this means is there is need for a lot of automation. This is automation that focuses not just on test suites but also automating test processes and efforts in all possible ways. For example, from the test suite standpoint, the team is looking at building scalable automation frameworks that can take on regression, compatibility, functionality, and performance testing, among others. From a test process standpoint, automated test deployments, automated defect and test case management, and automated metrics measurement and report generation are varied areas to consider. Automating the test processes is particularly a more cumbersome task. The reason is there are a lot of loose ends that can be easily done manually—due to this, there is resistance to adopting automation in such areas even among automation engineers. For example, a survey by Intersog shows 56% of bug tracking and 45% of defect closures happen manually.[3] Another piece of data shows only 25% of unit testing, 7% of integration testing, 5% of system testing, and 3% of acceptance testing are automated end to end. The data herein show 42% of automation tests are not automated. If we can automate these to reach near 100% of unattended executions, imagine the amount of time and cost savings that would result in a DevOps environment.

Typically some of the core problem areas impeding comprehensive automation include the disconnect between defect tracking and test case management and the need for coding skills to implement automation.

To this effect, in our organization, for example, we leverage something called adaptive test automation frameworks—these are frameworks that support the goal of building on automation to reduce manual tasks in all possible spheres of tester operations. This is a framework that encourages test case design and automation in human-readable format from within a defect, so that all pieces of the test effort are tightly coupled. The framework is also simple enough to encourage manual testers to take on automation. That said, now is the time for manual testers to spread their wings into the test automation space. While manual testing will not go away, a lot of focus will also be rightly given to the world of automation. Moving forward a tester can push himself only so much with manual testing skills. In the current times, automation is almost becoming inevitable. Figure 4.1 shows a simple workflow diagram of how the adaptive automation framework looks with test cases integrated within a defect management tool.

Besides enhanced automation, test has an added responsibility to take on root cause investigations to enable the rest of the product team fix issues faster and more completely. To be able to do this and think of deeper scenarios to test, it is becoming increasingly important for test to thoroughly understand the larger business of the organization and varied integration points with the product under test. While all of these have been traditionally recommended for test to take on even during the days of pure agile, these are becoming almost inevitable in the current days of DevOps.

Data show a sizeable growth in adoption of DevOps YoY. It has grown from 62% in 2014 to 66% in 2015.[4] This number will only rise in the coming years and whether or not your organization has moved to the world of DevOps, it will be a smart move for you to

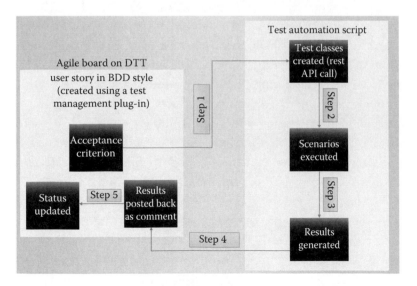

Figure 4.1   Adaptive test automation framework workflow.

already look at enhanced automation in your overall test effort and processes. And in this smart approach that teams are attempting to embrace, most of them are working their way up toward automation for existing feature sets leaving manual testing for primarily new user stories that come in to test. Even such new user stories soon make their way into the regression suite, forcing the need to be automated sooner or later.

What New Technologies Have Impacted the Overall Test Strategy and Effort?

In Chapter 2, we looked at influential factors that are driving a change in great detail. Technology was one such major bucket that we looked at. In this section, we will specifically talk about how varied technologies are impacting software testing and the kind of change they are bringing in.

Cloud

Even in the past period that we looked at in Chapter 3, cloud had a major influence on how we tested and what we tested. In the current times, this is only further intensifying with all systems being looked at from a services angle. For example, in the initial days, the cloud was all about software, platform, and infrastructure as a service. But today, this has taken shape in varied ways—for example, backend as a service. Similarly, with the growing concerns of public cloud, private cloud started gaining popularity a few years back. As with any technology or domain, the industry starts off with an extreme solution and soon settles for something middle ground. This is exactly what has been happening in the cloud space too, where we now have hybrid cloud evolving as a mix of both public and private clouds. This is a solution where organizations leverage the benefits of both the private and public offerings to decide which applications would be on the private segment, which would be on the public segment together building a combined cloud strategy. As for test, this calls for a combined test strategy too that focuses on the weaknesses of each of these areas. For example, for applications that are on the public cloud, the test focus is largely on the security and performance angles, while for the ones on private cloud, the focus is on customized feature implementations and rendering to yield the desired functionality at lowest possible costs. The growth in cloud, while it has provided a lot of flexibility for testers from a test engineering standpoint, has also expanded test opportunities and forced them to think of custom test strategies.

Mobile

Mobile computing is probably the biggest technology change that has greatly impacted the tester's realm of operations. Moving away from a desktop or laptop-based web application testing to a device or simulator/emulator-driven testing of web, native, or hybrid applications is a large change the testers are still getting used to. From a physical impact as well, testing on mobile devices with a handheld has been a big change. Obviously, it is just not a device that has brought in the change. The device in combination with an application development mind-set and the overall application development process has created a very large test impact. Mobile applications have brought in a lot of focus on nonfunctional testing elements such as performance, security, and usability. Newer business models around m-commerce and content digitization have all triggered new testing opportunities. In fact, it is interesting to see business strategies such as discounts being offered only on the mobile app, mobile shopping spree, and large retailers such as Flipkart in India working toward a mobile-only presence. Crowdsourced testing strategy has become more prevalent given the need to test applications on a large range of mobile devices across realistic user scenarios. The tester himself is now encouraged to think like an end user. Mobile testing is forcing testers to think deeper and bring out optimization opportunities—for example, we have a homegrown tool at QA InfoTech, called Mobile Application Strategy Tool. This is a tool that will help you consider varied parameters and weigh in on them to make suggestions on what kind of testing should be done to maximize overall test coverage with a minimal set of tests to be run. This will also help you make a call on where the tests should actually be run (whether on physical devices or on simulators through a crowd team). Figure 4.2 shows the pictorial view of the tool.

Mobile Application Strategy Tool

Step #1 | Problem Statement

Valid Alternative Decision Input Table

Step #2

Valid Alternatives	Evaluation Criteria					
Weights	0	0	0	0	0	0
Real devices						
Simulators/emulators						
Crowdsource platform						

Decision Analysis

Alternatives, Factors, and Weighted Scoring Appears Below Based upon the Input Provided Above

Step #3

Weighted Results						Total
Real devices	0	0	0	0	0	0
Simulators	0	0	0	0	0	0
Crowdsource platform	0	0	0	0	0	0

Figure 4.2 Pictorial view of MAST tool.

Additionally, testers are having to make smart optimization choices based on past analysis of test results to help them further strategize their mobile testing efforts. From our experience, here are some quick tips to empower testers with their mobile test efforts:

- Functional issues are more OS dependent rather than on the device size or screen resolution.
- User interface issues are more specific to a device size or screen resolution rather than OS.
- Different devices with the same screen size and OS version would give identical results.
- Devices with different screen size but identical OS version would give different results.

Wearable Computing and Augmented Reality

In continuation to mobile computing the next seen in the line is wearable computing and augmented reality. In very simple terms wearable computing is a wearable device with built-in computing capabilities that is able to render valuable information to end users across a range of functionalities. And augmented reality, whether it be mobile or nonmobile, is enhancing a real-life experience and augmenting it to provide relevant and timely information to end users in varied shapes and forms. Head-mounted displays and smart watches are popular examples of wearable devices that we are seeing in recent times. Testing for apps developed for wearable devices is a huge market and they come in not just as stand-alone apps that are tested but their computing elements that integrate with varied other apps and devices across the mobile and nonmobile segments. Similarly, testing for augmented reality apps calls for a number of pieces that integrate together and several out of box scenarios to be tried. Augmented reality is a very valuable discipline that also can add to a tester's toolkit enhancing his productivity rather than purely focusing on how to test augmented reality applications. The market for wearable computing is expected to touch $30 billion by 2018. Augmented reality, even for the nonmobile segment, is expected to touch $1 billion by the same time. Testing for these two segments requires a lot of out of box thinking—creative end-user scenarios, varied integration checks, and test areas that cover usability, compatibility, functionality, performance, etc. The tester also has to be aware of known limitations in these areas, since these are still evolving as we speak. For example, security is still a large unaddressed area in wearable computing. Surface detection is a gap in augmented reality. In newer areas such as these, the tester will have to also rely increasingly on community knowledge to determine what scenarios to additionally try. Crowdsourced testing to get end users to test is also very valuable. How to test augmented reality applications and also how to leverage augmented reality to enhance a tester's productivity are topics of their own, worth individual consideration.[5] Also, core testers may have to take on tests outside the traditional lab, as some scenarios may have to be tried on the field. Newer computing areas such as these are forcing testers to rethink their test strategy and the balance between manual and automated tests—while we understand the value of automated simulated tests, there is also tremendous value in field-driven manual testing. So, one of the questions to consider is whether advancements in technology are taking us to the grass roots of testing.[6]

Social Media

Social presence is not new. It has been influencing product development efforts significantly over the past decade, even more so in the last five years. What impact does social presence, be it your Facebook, Twitter, LinkedIn, Pinterest, or any other app, have on your testing effort? First thing to evaluate is whether your application or product under test has a social presence. If so, how you would test for it as a stand-alone app as well as an app in the social climate is something to plan to build into your test strategy. Additionally, in the current day, whether or not the application's functionality has a direct relevance to social media, there is a lot that the tester can seek from social media. All applications have a social face and users are very vocal on such mediums today. Their feedback, both positive and negative, is a great input to consider for additional testing in a given release or for enhancements in subsequent releases. Although the marketing team typically maintains the social presence of organizations and products, a tester can use this as an important source to understand the end-user satisfaction and overall product quality.

Analytics

This is certainly going to be the future for many more years to come. Today, it is all about user data. The volume of data handled in a sheer span of 60 seconds is mind-boggling. In 1 minute, e-mail users send 204 million messages, Amazon makes about $83,000 in online sales, and Apple users download 48,000 apps. On the social front, Facebook users share 2.46 million pieces of content, 277,000 tweets are tweeted, and Tinder users swipe left or right 416,667 times. All of these data are very valuable when analyzed and processed to bring relevance to core business. Organizations have started understanding this and a lot of emphasis is placed on analytics and big data to ensure the data are put to meaningful use. What this means is the tester now needs to understand how to test for such large data sets and ensure the right test coverage is obtained within the constraints of time and cost. The industry as a whole is grappling with testing big data and what tools to leverage, both to handle structured and unstructured data. From our experience, tools such as PigUnit and Hive under the larger Hadoop umbrella are the more popular ones that testers leverage today depending on what their usage needs may be. Table 4.1 is a very quick summary of these tools for you to consider depending on your requirements.

SMAC

Gradually the industry has gotten used to handling social, media, analytics, and cloud at individual levels. Teams have at varying levels understood what it takes to test them and how to incorporate results from each of those elements into the larger product context, which are all positive outcomes we are seeing. However, industry is

Table 4.1 Comparison of Big Data Tools

HIVE	PIG
Used by data analyst	Used by researchers and programmers
Used for completely structured data warehouse	Used for completely semistructured data warehouse
Declarative SQL language	Procedural data flow language
Used for creating reports	Used for programming

now moving into a newer trend—a trend called Social Media Cloud Analytics (SMAC) that brings together social, media, analytics, and cloud under one umbrella. This is a change at an organization level forcing companies to look for any missing pieces of the pie and fix them. For example, a given organization may have a strong mobile, analytical, and cloud presence but may miss the social piece. Now is the time such gaps are being taken care of. What this means for testers is 24 * 7 availability to address issues that surface. This stretches beyond the bounds of core testing and forces them to constantly evaluate information flowing in from users and how they are faring against competition and release live updates and patches on the go. The year 2014 had some interesting statistics to show. Seventy-six percent of businesses were using social media to fulfill their business goals, 72% acknowledged enhanced productivity through smart device adoption, 75% were focusing on leveraging analytics, and 92% were satisfied with outcomes from their cloud implementations.[7] These numbers are only going to further strengthen with the integration of these pieces to form the SMAC platform. As testers we need to continue to look for testing scenarios that tie in these pieces together to train ourselves to think from a holistic SMAC platform standpoint and what that interconnect means to overall product quality and market acceptance.

Computing Everywhere, Internet of Things, and Context-Sensitive Systems

The digital world today has become ubiquitous. Mobile penetration into remote parts of the world is on the rise. Internet availability, speeds, and reliability are improving by the day. With such strong infrastructure presence, businesses are looking at positively leveraging the user base and better connecting with them for relevant solutions. No longer is isolated solutioning taking place. Solutions are all coming together whether it be the SMAC that we saw previously or Internet of Things to bring in smart offerings or more importantly proactive user connect through context-sensitive systems. No longer is the user always reaching out to businesses with his requirements. An increasing trend is to see upsell where businesses have reached out to users with suggestions based on context they have about them. All of these mean the tester cannot limit his work to just his office premises. He lives and breathes quality even outside his core work hours, as you never know where one may get quality cues from. For example, I may be at a shopping mall or a restaurant over a weekend and may be able to see some live product users and get to interact with them. I may get an advertisement based on my set preferences that may give me cues for my product under test, say, when I am vacationing out of country. It is all about anywhere and anytime computing today and the tester who is able to connect the dots between what he does at work and what he sees outside when he is away from work is the one who will be able to thrive in the coming times. Just drawing the connection will also not suffice; he will have to translate them to actionable inputs that he can get back to his workplace to further enhance the quality of the product and bring in true business value.

The aforementioned list though not exhaustive is at least comprehensive enough to give you an idea of what is happening in the current times and how all of these are impacting testing. Other areas such as predictive analysis are also slowly making their way, all of which together are expected to bring in a huge change in the coming years in the world of software development. As a tester, it is important for us to understand and keep track of these to see how they relate to what we do currently and what else we can do differently, to experience ongoing continuous improvement.

The interesting takeaway here is that several testing best practices (e.g., think of nonfunctional areas, think like an end user) have all been long advocated in the testing industry—they continued to remain optional best practices all along. However, with the changes happening in technology today, they are slowly becoming inevitable best practices for teams to adopt.

What Other Things Are We Doing as Testers?

As a tester, we have come a long way. This period is one of most exciting yet challenging times that a tester is going through. Those who are able to handle and convert these challenges into opportunities clearly have a strong road laid ahead of them both for the products they are working on and for their own personal careers. What is driving all of this change? The state of product quality today, which in turn is directly influenced by state of product development, has a lot to do with what and what else we do as a tester. For instance, today product quality is no longer a responsibility of just the testing team. Obviously, if something goes wrong, it is still the testing team's neck that is out on line. But the rest of the teams have also started understanding and appreciating quality in hope of being able to contribute in possible ways within their spheres of operation. Secondly, the need for domain knowledge is more important now than ever before. As a tester, while my core testing skills of test planning, execution, and defect management are all important, now is the time I can differentiate myself with knowledge of the domain that I work on. This could be domain-specific workflows, regulations that govern the domain, market for the domain, etc. Additionally, although there are specific teams such as the business and marketing teams that are chartered with understanding market competition, a tester can add tremendous value in evaluating the current product against competition in areas such as feature set, functionality, performance, usability, and accessibility—all from a quality angle. And finally, it is becoming important for the tester to think beyond the bounds of his core testing work. Gone are the days where a tester comes in to execute his tests for 8 hours a day and at the end of the release signs off on his task set. Given the multitude of test scenarios, devices, and parameters that he works with, creativity is the need of the hour. We will look at what it takes for a tester to thrive in the current day, in a later section of this chapter, but at this time, we will specifically look at what other tasks a tester is taking on in addition to his core testing responsibilities.

Market Watcher

As a tester, today, it is important to live and breathe quality outside of core work hours too. One needs to be a keen market watcher to see how competition is faring—simple things such as what is the competition in the news for, what kind of feedback are users giving for the competition, what forums can I monitor to best gauge feedback for my own product, what are users' pain points, and are there any user-powered events that I can attend. These are all things that no one is going to direct a tester to take on. These need to be self-driven and those who do these are able to clearly set themselves apart.

Innovation Seeker

Innovation has become the key to thrive in any discipline and testers are no exceptions. We are seeing testers do amazingly different things to enhance their productivity and also add to the quality of the product whether it be newer tools and frameworks, bringing in newer concepts such as games into software testing, keeping track of new technologies, etc. Innovation need not be something very big to get noticed—testers are even taking on small steps and are eventually seeing a difference in what they do. Management teams are also more receptive to such continuous improvement strategies than ever before, creating a very conducive environment overall for the quality landscape.

Quality Empowering Collaborator

A tester is often seen helping the rest of the product team take on quality in possible spaces of their work. For example, he is helping a developer with unit test case creation and execution of sanity automated tests to ensure the build released to test is more reliable. Similarly, he is seen working with the operations teams with a sanity suite of tests to ensure live issues from the field are better responded to with a tighter service-level agreement (SLA). When he takes on such tasks to empower others on the team own quality, he is indirectly creating a stronger base for himself to take on bigger and better tasks since the core and tactical tasks are now handled across the team rather than just by himself.

Doubling on One's Role

Typically, as testers we tend to specialize in a core area—for instance, functional testing, performance testing, and security testing. While the core specialization still remains, in today's scenario the ones who are able to take on more as a value add to their core tasks are able to do even better in their role as software testers. For instance, at QA InfoTech, we recently introduced a couple of frameworks based on open-source tools—one is a framework where a functional tester is able to double on his open-source selenium scripts to take on not just functional testing but also security testing based on Open Web Application Security Project (OWASP) standards although he may not be a security expert and the other where a functional tester is able to take on accessibility testing. It is a good idea in general to get a cross perspective of the product and branch into other test types too in addition to your niche that you may be specializing in. For instance, given how the mobile application market is skyrocketing and how users react adversely to poor usability experience, an area to consider is how non-usability testers can take on usability testing too. This need not be very complex—it could be simple ones such as evaluating the product from an end-user experience, error scenarios, and overall application simplicity and workflow standpoints. When we do this as a tester, we are able to bring in better customer appreciation.

While all of the newer tasks we take on outside our traditional role of a tester are indeed exciting, there is one glitch that needs to be carefully evaluated. All of these require close collaboration with the rest of the team and sometimes even delegation of responsibilities from a tester's plate to another. When these are done without careful and insightful planning, mindful of the other entities involved we may appear to be trespassing into another team's area of operations. If and when such a thought process creeps into the team, the overall collaboration tends to be more destructive than constructive. Thus, a tester is required not just to excel in his own zone of operations but really look for opportunities to bond with the team and excel as a group, savvy for team's sensitivities that need to be balanced with quality goals and market requirements.

We Are at the Crossroads

With all of this multifold responsibility on a tester's plate today, he is really at a crossroad. A well-respected tester in the fraternity, James Bach, calls out seven different types of testers: an administrative tester who is very process oriented, technical tester who is very tools and frameworks driven, an analytical tester who is very logical and statistical in his test approach, a social tester who is very embracing of his team and other entities in his test efforts, a developer tester who is very detail oriented at a programming level, a user expert who is keen to track user feedback, and finally an empathetic tester who again empathizes not just with users but is mindful of all entities at stake. There is no right or wrong approach here on who you should be; also, you need not contain yourself to just one type of tester. What is important though is for testers to see which of these profiles best defines who they are today and whether that is sufficient for them to be in, in the coming days for their market and their own career aspirations. Accordingly, they need to look for diversification opportunities to branch into newer tester types.

As someone who is doing over and above what has traditionally been expected of them, a tester should not lose focus of certain core elements. These are elements that will help both him and his product succeed—and cover the need to accommodate context, collaboration, customer, competition, and company in whatever we do. We need to continuously evaluate and align our actions with these five "Cs" (Figure 4.3) to ensure there is overall return on investments in our efforts.

As for the kinds of tests we run as a tester today, at the very core not much has changed since the past. What is changing is how we run the tests and how we prioritize them. While functional testing continues to be important, nonfunctional test areas such as performance, security, usability, and accessibility are becoming increasingly important today. End users are paying equal importance to these areas. An application, despite how rich it may be in its functionality, if lacking on its performance, for example, its responsiveness, will

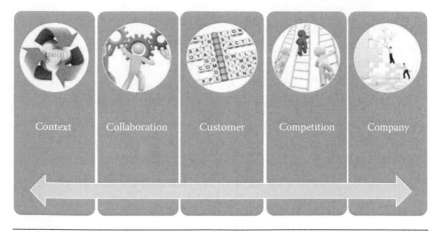

Figure 4.3 5C strategy to organizational success.

lose ground to its competition. This wasn't as prominent in the past, when the market was limited to a few large enterprise players. Given that situation has changed now, where users have ample options to go with, organizations are placing heavy emphasis to nonfunctional test areas as well. A scalable and equipped test lab has become inevitable to support test execution across a range of devices. In specific scenarios not all devices can be stocked in house due to constraints around device cost, availability, usage, etc. In such cases, additionally where there is value in bringing in end-user context in the test effort, testers are leveraging crowd users to test applications. These are often freelance testers who are brought in to test given their domain expertise, end-user experience, or niche value addition in areas such as localization, accessibility, and usability.

Also as testers, we are changing strategies on how we test. For example, we are increasingly moving toward test automation. Newer emphasis is placed on techniques such as exploratory testing and bug bashes to enable teams bring out their creative best within the shortest possible test cycles. Test cases that are designed are more in a human-readable (behavior-driven) format. For example, they all may consistently have a format such as "GWT—Given When Then." When such consistent formats are used, it also becomes easier to bring in modular test automation that is more understandable even among nonprogrammers.

In terms of evaluation, test teams are getting more objective in measuring outcomes. Outcomes are mapped to overall coverage and traceability to the defined requirements. Connecting tests run to user stories, the coverage obtained in terms of code coverage, the kind of defects reported, percentages of valid defects, how defects were found, who found the defects and when they were found, feedback coming in from end users, and team's adherence to defined SLAs for quality and performance are all becoming increasingly used. While it has been important in the past to keep track of tests run by the tester to understand how productive he was, today, productivity is measured by other parameters. What kind of new utilities did someone bring in to the team, any new practices that made the team's work smarter, and how a tester has been contributing to doing things differently are all used as gauges to understand his performance and productivity. This is all a welcome change and a much needed facelift to truly map test metrics to understand the quality of the product, the quality of the test effort, and the performance of a tester. This is a big change from how things were done in the past. So, organizations and testers alike will need to understand and implement these metrics in the true spirit to derive ongoing value, and when such a mature state is reached, it will certainly be an exciting time for the testing fraternity as a whole.

Case Studies

As in the previous chapter, I would like to share a couple of representative case studies for your understanding on the kind of work we do today and how they align with the various topics we have discussed in this chapter. These are case studies from QA InfoTech, where my teams have had to go the extra mile in custom designing a solution for the client or think out of box for an out-of-norm solution given the kind of technical challenges that are thrown at a tester today. The first case study talks about a complex compatibility test effort that we took on and the second as to how we handled test automation for a flash application with a combination of open-source tools. In both cases, it shows how the test team had to go out of its traditional comfort zone to solve client issues in a limited period of time.

Case Study 1

Cover Note and Client Overview Device compatibility testing has increased testing scope leaps and bounds in the recent years. A state of preparedness to take on device compatibility testing at short notice is becoming inevitable. Here's a case study on how we did this for a client, bringing in more coverage than they had expected.

Our client is one of the pioneers in providing niche services in health-care educational domain. They are an online leader in nursing education. They produce a variety of unique print and digital content, learning tools, etc., to prepare professionals for the nursing industry. They are involved in assisting universities and businesses in educating and nurturing talent in the health-care domain.

Challenges and Need   The client has an online learning portal that runs only on desktop browsers since it was created with Silverlight tool.

They created a newer version of the application and wanted to release the Silverlight-independent application to cater to the generation of smart mobile device users.

A fully tested application was to be rolled out to the new category of users.

They wanted to have maximum coverage across devices and OS/browser combinations.

Also they wanted to ensure that the transition of the existing user base to the application's new UI is smooth.

The newly designed UI product would be available firstly for devices greater than 7″ screen size.

Solution   We at QA InfoTech have a varied inventory of devices covering a range of compatibility matrices. Our inventory consists of various devices ranging from Windows XP, Windows 7, and Windows 8 in different machine configurations to Macintosh, UNIX, and a wide variety of smartphone devices used by different categories of users so that we provide a realistic experience of testing rather than using simulators.

We first started off creating a matrix in which we listed all the OSs that the client had promised to support the product in. We ensured that all browsers compatible with the OS were covered in that matrix. We then listed all the smart devices ranging from tablets with Android, iOS, Kindle Fire, Kindle Fire HD, and Surface. We also made sure that we had the devices across different screen sizes ranging from 7″ to 10″.

The entire test plan and effort was documented through Zephyr—a plug-in tool available in JIRA.

Approach   We first confirmed the adequacy of the compatibility matrix we had created, with the product owner. They were excited that our planned coverage was more than what they had expected. Additionally, since we had the inventory of all these devices, we could start the effort right away.

We then created a detailed regression test cycle for the application and wrote test cases covering each functionality and executed them under the compatibility test cycle for each sprint.

We also had created a smoke checklist separately in Zephyr and ensured that we executed it under compatibility testing cycle in addition to the release specific cycle.

Steps Carried Out for Each Release   Executed the regression and the compatibility checklists and signed off on QA.

Executed the smoke checklist under compatibility test cycle for the specific release providing live sign-off.

There is a "Feedback" feature available on the application where each end user can input the problems faced and submit it with details. The feature is integrated with JIRA. Each entered feedback gets created as a separate entry in JIRA. Due to the wide variety of smart devices that we have at QA InfoTech, this task was also assigned to us to ensure that we review, regress, and take care of each individual feedback.

Client Benefits   With the previously defined solution, we were able to cover the entire range of smart devices and helped our client support and target a large customer base.

Also, due to the creation of segregated regression, smoke checklist, and execution under compatibility cycle in Zephyr along with regression cycle, we could ensure the release covered the compatibility matrix in its entirety during the cycle window.

Although the release window was widened, the greatest advantage was we were able to ensure that the build going live had the maximum possible compatibility coverage.

The client was very happy with this effort as OS/browser coverage in the release window brought in better test and release confidence. Also, the wider range of devices available in our inventory helped the client in efficient review and quicker issue triaging.

We helped in identifying the root cause of the issue and providing quicker solutions to the issues. This eventually helped them in saving quality time.

Case Study 2

Cover Note and Client Overview

 Automating a Flash Application Flash content undoubtedly gives a lot of richness to applications that are designed. However, from a tester standpoint there are challenges to handle, as not all test automation tools support flash-based automation. Discussed here is a case study of a custom test automation framework that we created for one of our clients that had flash-powered applications.

Client Our client is a global leader in the E-learning domain. The company provides superior content, personalized services, and course-driven digital solutions that accelerate student engagement and transform the learning experience.

 Their main focus is "Engagement," that is, engaging with learners, both in the classroom and beyond, to ensure the most effective product design, learning solutions, and personalized services are delivered.

Challenges We were required to automate one of the modules that had a lot of repetitive functionality requiring more than 6 hours of manual QA efforts to smoke test.

 The challenge was that this module was developed in flash. Developers use flash to make their websites rich and interactive, but it poses a lot of challenges with test automation as selenium web-driver tool (commonly used in open-source test automation) cannot read or record any actions on flash objects.

 There were two key questions that had to be addressed while automating the application linking flash objects:

1. Authenticating a certain value is set—where you need to "get" certain properties of the object and compare it against your benchmarks
2. Executing actions on an object or "set" certain values

Solution We typically use selenium web driver as an open-source tool to automate HTML page objects. As this module is developed in flash and the selenium web driver fails to identify its objects, we needed a tool that could automate flash page objects. Sikuli was our new tool of choice and we integrated it with selenium. Sikuli is an image-based automation tool in which actions and verifications are based on images—although image-based automation is not the best solution, this in combination with selenium addressed our needs of flash-based test automation.

Approach   We developed an automation framework that was an integration of various tools and technologies including selenium web driver, Sikuli, FitNesse, Java, Fixtures, HTML, and XML. This consolidated framework is capable of using selenium web driver and Sikuli to smartly identify HTML and flash contents. This framework is based on a data-driven approach where we have created test code in sync with the data set within the framework. It enables execution of flash modules with different combinations of data inputs and also brings in the benefits of code reusability, test code coverage, and reproducible test results. This approach also helped us maintain the test script without much overhead.

Steps

1. Developed a selenium-based test automation framework
2. Integrated Sikuli and FitNesse with the framework
3. Integrated sequence fixtures with the framework
4. Identified and stored all images for flash page objects used by Sikuli during the automation workflows
5. Created resource files to be used by the script at run time
6. Added HTML and XML plug-ins within framework to generate customized reports
7. Also added plug-ins to export results as PDF files

Client Benefits   With this solution, we were able to automate the application that had flash content and execution time was also reduced to less than 2 hours. Also, we were able to execute the automated scripts on two machines simultaneously—smoke tests were thus completed in less than an hour during releases.

Client was very excited with the outcome, as it helped bring down test effort time and cost, brought in E2E test automation, and more importantly handled automated flash content that would not have been possible without out of box solutions.

How Do We Thrive in Today's Environment?

When drastic changes roll out in any discipline, the players often feel threatened. The sense of insecurity due to fear of the unknown is very high. With the evolution of DevOps and the focus on greater auto-mation, testers in the recent years have been sailing a similar boat—a boat where they are unsure if their role is still valuable and whether their position will continue to prevail. So, more than a question of thriving, for several of them it has even been a question of surviving. Having been in the independent software testing business for over 12 years now and having worked with a range of clients, Fortune and start-ups alike, the reassurance I want to give to the community is that testing is here to stay—quality assurance and confirmation have a bright future. That said, like in any other discipline, complacency will get an individual only so far. This is sometimes called the Fat, Dumb, and Happy syndrome, especially in large organizations where employ-ees get very comfortable with what they do, jeopardizing both their own careers and the company's external positioning in a few years. To ensure a healthy, competitive environment and to continue to thrive at a fraternity level, it is important for the testers to keep a few things in mind. These are fairly self-explanatory, so I will list them as points:

1. Look for newer challenges to solve either initiated by your team or at a self-inflicted level.
2. Leverage technology not just in what you test but also how you test. For instance, use cloud to empower your test pro-cesses and analytics to help sift through the volumes of test data and draw meaningful inferences.
3. Ensure you along with people from other teams review your own work. Similarly, be closely involved in reviewing the work of other teams. This not only ensures all grounds are covered but also creates strong team bonding.
4. Be in close communication with the management to translate your tactical actions into strategic quality decisions.

5. Focus on strengthening your test environment and toolkit to ensure you are empowered to be productive.
6. Build an ongoing learning plan on a range of topics—testing processes, tools, trends, technologies, etc.—and have a custom list of feeds that you use for each of these.
7. Have trust in yourself and inspire such trust among people around you.

Current Trends That Will Also Set the Base Moving Forward

Trends define what is coming in the foreseeable future. Not all trends may take off at the same intensity, but trends definitely give a great insight to plan for the future and be prepared for what is in store. We are almost at the close of the "current period" under consideration. In the next chapter we will start looking at the future of testing, which will cover the base for 2016 and beyond. To prepare for what is coming, let's wrap up this chapter looking at what those trends are that define the coming years. Since we have discussed most of these points in great detail at varied places in this chapter, I will herein just wrap up and summarize the trends as takeaways for this chapter and the premise for the next chapter:

1. Technology landscape is very dynamic today.
2. Application development on mobile platforms will continue to grow.
3. Mobile-only renderings will soon enter the scene, making desktop-based web applications a thing of the past.
4. End users will have an increasing role in software development—more crowdsourced testing will prevail.
5. The existence of independent testing will be challenged, but will prevail.
6. Commercial and open-source tools will coexist and become more collaborative unlike the current time, where they were seen actively competing against each other.
7. A shift left to understand system internals and a shift right to align with end users will have to be the balance in strategy for a tester to take in.

8. DevOps will see increasing levels of automation but will continue to embrace manual testing into its fold—manual testers will see an increased need to branch into test automation.

9. Testing centers of excellence will grow to cross share knowledge and resources and to build on efficiencies.

10. Testers will be increasingly respected for their role in upholding quality and bringing the team together toward a common goal holding end-user requirements high.

11. QA/tester's toolkit on one hand is strengthening but on the other is becoming lighter. This is a great trend to see where the toolkit only has really valuable tools that testers can repeatedly use. Some of the low-value tools are taken a close look at and removed from the set to include tools that are more powerful and oftentimes multifaceted in what they offer.

12. Compliance-based testing (Section 508, HIPAA, SOX, among others) will continue to rise giving a formal need for independent validation and verification.

How Is a Tester's Career Shaping Today?

A tester's career today is more exciting than ever in the past. I say this as opportunities are abound. However, these are not always easy and straightforward opportunities. Gone are the days when a tester could afford to sit reactively and wait for opportunities to come along his way. Today, he has to chalk his own career path and go beyond the bounds of what his manager may define for him. When he does this, the industry is ready to welcome him with open arms in varied areas of niche specialization that align with his interests and capabilities. Outside his core test team, the other entities from whom he can take in inputs include his product team, stakeholders, end users, and market entities—be it forums, conferences, end users, discussion groups, social media, etc. With such vital sources of information, a tester's career today has become one that he can shape or destroy himself—both are in his own hands and now is the opportune moment for those with the zeal to make the best use of what the opportunities have got to offer. Management is also very receptive to suggestions and inputs coming in from all entities. A tester's career today is not merely dependent on what he does but also how he represents it to the relevant people. He thus needs to both be able to "walk the talk" and "talk the walk" to ensure he has an edge in the market and is able to truly deliver on products of exceptional quality. When all of these fall in place, automatically his career progression would have been taken care of along the way. Additionally, all of what we have discussed in this chapter—be it "how to thrive" or "what trends are we seeing"—are all actionable inputs for the tester to work on toward giving his career a positive facelift.

Did You Know?

1. Software testing industry is today a $13 billion industry.[8]
2. Mobile application testing numbers are soaring by the year. The percent of organizations practising mobile application testing has increased from 31 in 2012 to 55 in 2013 to 87 in 2014 and is expected to touch 95 by the end of 2015.[9]
3. The test budget for new development projects exceeds that of maintenance projects for the first time since 2012: from 41% in 2012 to 52% in 2014.[10]
4. The test portion in IT budgets continues to rise—from 18% in 2012 to 26% in 2014. Thirty-five percent of organizations however state they aren't satisfied with the budget allocated to testing.[3]

References

1. Lakein, A. http://www.brainyquote.com/quotes/quotes/a/alanlakein154655.html?src=t_present.
2. DevOpsGuys. 2013. http://blog.devopsguys.com/2013/12/19/the-top-ten-devops-operational-requirements/.
3. http://intersog.com/blog/automated-software-testing-2015-adoption-tools-and-other-trends/.
4. Bourne, J. 2015. http://www.cloudcomputing-news.net/news/2015/feb/18/devops-adoption-rises-and-hybrid-cloud-strategy-deepens-new-study/.
5. Test Huddle Admin. 2015. http://testhuddle.com/resource/the-connect-between-augmented-reality-and-software-testing/.
6. Padmanaban, R. 2013. https://www.techwell.com/techwell-insights/2013/03/new-technology-taking-us-back-grassroots-software-testing.

7. https://www.epam.com/ags-is-now-part-of-epam.
8. Testbytes. 2015. http://www.evoketechnologies.com/blog/software-testing-trends-predictions-2015/.
9. http://testbytes.net/blog/top-5-software-testing-trends-to-look-out-for-in-2015/.
10. https://www.capgemini.com/thought-leadership/world-quality-report-2014-15.

5

WHAT DOES THE FUTURE BEHOLD FOR SOFTWARE TESTING?

Even though the future seems far away, it is actually beginning right now.

—Mattie Stepanek[1]

Tomorrow is already a thing of the future. In any discipline, one cannot push out or avoid the future for very long, saying it is yet to come—as this quote rightly says, it is actually beginning right now. And as you have been reading this book all along, my goal is to help the reader connect the dots between chapters by already introducing you into what such future beholds so that you can work on getting yourself ready for it. I concluded in Chapter 4 with trends to watch for and what is coming up next. We will discuss those in greater detail in this chapter. As you are aware, we will have a separate chapter to talk about what this means to the testing fraternity as a whole and to testers' careers so we will exclusively talk about how things will change in this profession in the coming years, in this chapter.

We Will Start Off by Talking about a Very Controversial Question: "Is Testing Dying and Will It Cease to Exist in the Coming Years?"

There is no direct answer to this question, except to strongly say that all lies in the perspective of the testing group that is involved. If the team happens to be one that is content with its current style of operations and is complacent or not willing to move on and align with the changing needs, then yes, I can strongly say testing will die soon. But if the fraternity at large and testing teams at their small levels understand the changing facets of software quality and work toward customizing and adopting them in their own spaces of operation in possible ways, the future not only exists but is also bright. Such agility is the need of the day today and into the future to ensure quality is built into the products up front. Today, release cycles have already shrunk from several months to just several weeks for many products. This will only continue to further shrink in the coming years necessitating quality to be absolutely nimble. However, since quality has become and will continue to be a collective ownership of the team, the test team will have to create its own value proposition to continue to position itself on the team. Also, they need to take on bigger and better tasks, primarily focusing on continuous integration and delivery, which means more overall automation (both at a test case and at a process level). If as a fraternity we are able to do this, test will not be a dying profession but definitely a thriving profession with a much better facelift and positioning than what it has today.

The Dynamic Landscape Will Continue to Become Increasingly Dynamic

The influential factors we have been talking about at varied places in this book will continue to strengthen, making the landscape even more dynamic than ever before. Technology is becoming omnipresent. There is hardly any discipline today that is untouched by technology. Also mobile, social, cloud, and analytics-based computing will continue to engulf all new areas that technology is seeping into. Continuous integration and delivery will make the development landscape completely dynamic, forcing the team members to be in an ever-ready state to take on tasks on demand. Such dynamism is not just individual driven but also process and effort driven, making this the most important trait for the entire team to inculcate in the coming times.

App Development Will Soar

Mobile app development will reach newer heights. As of October 2015, just in the U.S. Apple Store, the number of active applications to download was close to two million. While games, education, business, and entertainment are some of the top categories for app development, newer areas especially such as health care and fitness are all soon catching up. The market is very bullish where anyone with a novel idea can see it take shape with ample resources available to build the application. That being the case, these numbers will only continue to soar—app development will not stop with just mobile devices. Wearables and augmented reality powered devices will also bring in their own apps, making this a huge market. Testing will have to align with this growth since in many cases even leading retailers may choose to offer just an app rendering rather than a web application. All of this calls for a completely different mobile strategy—the one that is very collaborative to pool in devices and other test resources at short notice, even requiring a very active pool of crowd testers to be maintained. More than the test effort itself, the testing teams will have to showcase a state of being ever ready as most test passes may even just last for a day or so. This is something we are already seeing today and will continue to intensify in the coming times, making it inevitable for testers to be on their feet and able to take on tasks on demand.

Testers Will Coexist with Crowd Users

As we move ahead in the world of software development and testing, the lines the tester holds with varied entities will blur and one such group is that of the end users. Increasingly, testers will collaborate and communicate with end users not just to get their feedback but also to leverage them as crowd users. Gone past are the days when testers felt threatened with such external entities coming in raising a sense of insecurity about their own job. Testers now understand the value crowd users bring in and how that will help them further improve the quality of the product under test. They will increasingly understand that with unique value propositions that each of the groups bring in, they will together be able to ship the product sooner and with the desired levels of quality. Even if this crowd tester base is not directly the end-user base, there will be crowd testers who are domain specialists and other testers themselves from across the world who will help bring in additional test coverage through their efforts.

Testing Fraternity Will Work to Seek Balance in a Number of Areas

Gone are the days when you as a tester will take on everything on your plate and work in an isolated manner. Today, the need of the day is the act of balancing—balancing efforts between several groups of people, balancing practices, processes, tools, etc., all with the common goal of product quality. This will further get intensified in the coming days where the tester will have to work smart in striking balance across multiple variables. For example, testers will increasingly take on the balancing act between the following:

- What they do and what the crowd testers do including what, when, and how to engage crowd testers.
- What coverage to achieve on real devices and what should be done on emulators and simulators.
- When to use commercial tools and when to use open source tools—Herein, while the debate goes on at an industry level as to which one is better than the other, the new trend is for each of these groups to acknowledge, embrace the other, and coexist. For example, at a panel discussion we were part of, in the UNICOM conference in India in 2015, the topic under debate was exactly this. It was welcoming to see the commercial tool group talk about their contributions to the open source world, and the open source world acknowledge that sometimes they build their solutions on commercial tools. Today, both sides understand their strengths and weaknesses and such awareness is great for the industry at large to benefit from.
- When to merge and collaborate with the rest of the team members and when to work in isolation to retain their independence.

Increasing Collaboration in All We Do

In all of this coexistence, the act of balancing will make testing not just an act of quality assurance and confirmation but an act of collaboration. We will increasingly become social testers who collaborate well with varied entities helping us cross share responsibilities, ownerships, and tasks. Testers and the rest of the product teams will become increasingly mature to understand and see such collaboration in positive light rather than being intimidated as being trespassed by other entities.

Manual Testing Will Not Disappear but Will Become Completely Niche

As testers, the one other question we often hear today is whether manual testing will disappear in the coming days. While it is true that a lot more automation will become mainstream given the world of DevOps we are moving into, manual testing will not cease to exist. With the changes in technology and newer applications of such technology, for example, wearable computing, a lot of field testings will be necessitated in the coming days. Such testings will require more manual testing. Exploratory testing will become increasingly valuable that will largely be done manually. What is important to understand is that manual testing will be limited to the core minimum, while the rest will move into an automated mode. A manual tester will have to elevate himself to learn the art of automation, too. Those remaining in the manual testing field will be the more experienced, select few that can take on very-high-end manual tasks of connecting their efforts with the larger business goals, test strategy, and planning. The lower-end manual test tasks are what will cease to exist. Thus, it is important to accept what will go away and what will remain so testers can train themselves accordingly for the coming days.

Nonfunctional Areas Will Become Very Important
Including Compliances Related to Them

As users become increasingly connected with the product under development, their expectations from the product go up. That is exactly where we are today and will increasingly move into, in the coming days. This trend will necessitate a greater push toward nonfunctional testing. Performance, security, accessibility, usability, and localization will all become very important areas to test for in line with the priorities of core functional testing. Government-mandated compliances and standards will increasingly be enforced for nonfunctional test areas to bring in consistency in software development. There will also be domain-specific mandates in areas such as banking, health care, and insurance. We are already seeing mandates such as Sec 508, DDA, SOX, and HIPAA, which will further be enforced, and newer ones will enter the market to make it all increasingly regulated and focused on the experience yet safety of the end users.

Automation Will Become an Increasingly Integral Part of Software Testing

The current ongoing push to automate more will only further rise in the coming days. The talk is all about automation today and it certainly is not baseless. In the world of DevOps that we operate in, the amount of direct human involvement needs to be minimized to just the core strategic tasks. Everything else needs to be automated. Manual testers at the lower end of the software testing career pyramid must ramp up their test automation efforts; failing to do so may stall their careers very soon. The idea in all of this is to automate to the largest possible extent so as to leave time for core tasks such as test strategizing, user connect, exploratory testing, and monitoring the entire test process to keep the engine flowing smoothly. And even in test automation, the push will increasingly move toward reuse as much as possible. For example, can my functional test scripts also be used for other purposes such as security testing and accessibility testing, are my tests fully automated or am I still doing certain tasks manually, are my tests integrated well with my test case and defect management tools, etc.? Also, in cases such as health care and such other critical software, it will become important to simulate and automate as much as possible as real-life testing may not even be possible. If one were to look at what is that one big change software testing will see in the coming years, it is the steep rise in test automation, both test execution and test process automation.

*Agile Will Become a No-Brainer but Customizations
Are What Teams Will Need to Understand*

Development teams including test teams are already used to the agile style of development. This is a no-brainer where we now understand what it takes to deliver the agile way. Fast time to market, reduced cost of operations, focus on quality, end user–focused development are all well understood and appreciated today. The need for these will be further intensified in the coming days. Today, continuous integration and delivery is not very widely adopted. While the awareness exists, adoption is still very low. This will change in the coming days. Teams will not only embrace these concepts but will increasingly work on customized models to align with their market and user needs. As for quality, this will mean on-demand work. The automation suite has to be robust, scalable, of high quality, and maintainable that tests can be run anytime and can be invoked from anywhere. Customizations and changes will happen even between releases within the same product to get the teams more ready to meet the market needs. Agility will become a norm in team's operations, people's mind-set, and for that matter anything that is done that teams are in a state of ever readiness to tackle any situation. This will make them both proactive and effectively reactive, to cut an edge for themselves in the market.

Testing Will Not Be Confined to Just Your Core
Hours of Work in Office Premises

Everyone wants a work–life balance, right? Who doesn't? However, with the way software development and quality is shaping, it will soon become very difficult to confine testing to just 8 hours of work in the office premises. In a lot of testing, use case scenarios will happen on mobile devices, which is integral to all of our daily lives today. That being said, a tester will increasingly see connections between his or her core work and his or her life outside work, in the future. For instance, the tester may have several touch points to the app's social presence even when he is outside work. At a social event, for instance, he may meet users of the product. The tester has to be ever ready to seek and take feedback for the product even when he is not at office, and the touch points he will have, to do this will only continue to rise in the coming years.

Will Metrics Still Be Used? For Such Short Releases,
How Do We Connect the Dots with the Past?

These are valid questions the testing community will face. Given how short the release cycles are, the testers hardly have any time to take on the test effort. If so, where do they have time to analyze the data, draw inferences, and make meaningful decisions? This is where the testing community has to get smarter. We need to pick and choose only the most relevant metrics (not even the ones that the industry is using at large but the ones that are relevant to our product and market) and again automate them to make the process easy and less cumbersome for everyone to adopt, given the time constraint on hand.

Independent Testing's Future

As testers, we have gone through a lot of ordeal in the last two decades to establish a status of independent testing. The last decade has been especially challenging as we try to understand and create awareness on what independent testing is all about and how to achieve it in the world of collaborative software development. Testers have had to tread a very fine line to maintain the role delineation between them and the developers. This will get increasingly challenging in the coming years given the kind of development efforts that are coming into the mainstream mode. For instance, with a lot of app development, we see a lot of freelance developers across the globe. These are often people who wear multiple hats including that of the ideator, designer, developer, tester, operations, and support. In all of this mix, the sanctity of independent testing is bound to be lost. As a fraternity, we need to be aware of this risk and watch out to ensure independent testing is applied in areas we are involved in. This is a much larger responsibility that extends beyond just the testing fraternity. The software development community at large will need to understand the risk and potential repercussions involved to ensure independent testing is given the positioning it deserves. A very detailed section on the state of independent testing is discussed in the next chapter on the state of a tester's readiness.

The Merge between Development Testing and Software Testing

Elaborating on the previous point, given how testers are collaborating with the rest of the members of the product teams, the ones with whom they will collaborate the most is that of the developers. The collaboration will extend beyond discussing user scenarios, test coverage, defects, etc., but to possible areas of overlap in the work as well. For example, small issues, defects in areas such as localization, and content may easily be fixed by the tester himself rather than having to go through the full loop with the team. Testers will work with developers and operations team to enable them take on automated test runs to help build quality much earlier into the development life cycle. In cases such as these, there is a clear and cognizant overlap that the cross teams buy into, to help each other for the benefit of the overall product under development.

A Twist to Testing Centers of Excellence (TCoE)

Traditionally, the term TCoE is not new. As testers, we know that TCoE, especially in large organizations with a huge quality effort, helps bring in testers to load balance their efforts, share resources, and take up knowledge transfer to bring in economies of scale and operations. Specialized testers were cross shared, buffer testers would reside in a pool to be leveraged as and when a team needs them, cross training would happen, etc. However, in the current day, teams are so busy and occupied on an ongoing basis, in which it has become important for all of these to be resident to specific teams rather than common to a TCoE. While the model of TCoE itself will only further grow in the coming years, the reasons why TCoE will be leveraged will be quite different from the past. Given how testers are busy in collaborating and working with the rest of the team, TCoE will be more of a spring board for them to fall back on, huddle together with fellow testers, and exchange best practices and lessons learned. It will almost become a parent's home to a kid that has branched out to go meet and work with the rest of the entities—it will be both a learning place and a feel good, morale boost abode for them to come back to, at periodic intervals. If the team at large understands the goal of such TCoEs, which may even exist virtually and remotely, there is tremendous value to be reaped from such an implementation, in the coming years especially to standardize testing efforts at an organization and industry level.

In summary, testing will move into a faster pace roller-coaster mode, much faster than it has ever been in the past. If we talk about releases that are going to be as short as one day, how do we as testers decide what kinds of tests need to be run? We are also talking about the importance of nonfunctional areas, the need to automate, the need to think beyond user stories, and stretching to be a tester beyond core work hours. If all of these mean the tester is doing much more than before and the time is much less than before, is it all really a fair share of tasks on the tester's plate? This question will equally apply to other entities on the team as well, as we are all expected to do much more in much less time—this is now an active call for all entities on the team to be effective at what we do and look for ways of continuous improvement, so we are able to gear up for what the future holds and have an edge both for ourselves and for our organization and product.

As we gear for this new era in software testing, I want to discuss one case study of such a futuristic project that we are working on at quality assurance (QA) InfoTech to give you a sense of the kind of work we are seeing currently and how the team is gearing up to face these challenges and new opportunities. Given the importance of this topic, we will dedicate two chapters related to this subject—one of whether the testing fraternity is ready for this change and another on what all of these mean to software testers—in the following sequence.

And before we move on to them, here is a case study of a challenging futuristic project that we are working on and how we are handling the quality assurance efforts for this client.

Cover Note and Client Overview

Shaping Up the Future of QA in the Evolving Technology Space

With the paradigm shift from iterative models to agile and now DevOps, there is a sea change in the go-to-market strategy with lot of emphasis on quick, reliable releases and continuous delivery. This results in a lot of forward and backward integration in the overall development processes to ingrain agility, flexibility, and reliability. A lot of new tools and path-breaking practices are being developed around continuous delivery to find every possible way to optimize the overall development and delivery process. Keeping in line with this, the QA function all together is reinventing itself. But this is also bringing up questions about the QA function: Is it an impediment? Or a necessary evil? Or an enabling and value-adding function to the overall development process? This case study provides insights into one such client where the QA function has gone through a strategic change with the changing times and needs.

Client

The client is a global leader in the e-learning domain, especially in health-care sector and certifications. The company provides superior content, government-regulated course material for nurses, and other

medical professionals and course-driven digital solutions that accelerate student engagement and transform the learning experience.

Challenges

- *Production releases frequently rolled back*: The product platform
  is huge and complex, with a lot of integrated components,
  communicating with each other. Development and fixes to
  one component need extensive testing across full platform to
  validate any impact. Most components have ongoing changes
  handled by separate project teams. Comprehensive regression
  tests for platform before any release had become inevitable.
  The rush against completing the extensive platform regression
  tests within available time resulted in leakages and production rollbacks.
- *Reliability of regression tests*: Due to enormity of tests and lack
  of a directly visible linkage between requirements/features
  and tests, confidence on regression tests was low. Also, with
  ongoing sprints, there was never a time when all tests could be
  run on the final build. There was always a huge freeze period
  on staging to enable running tests and fixing defects, thus
  thwarting integration of newer developments.
- *Repeated elaborate deployment planning and delayed production
  deployment schedule*: Due to enormity of the platform with
  lack of integrated build process, deployment planning always
  came out as a mammoth task—this resulted in further delays
  to the deployment process.
- *Frequent post deployment issues*: With pressure on releases in
  agile environment and changes taken in until the last moment,
  regression tests could never be reliably executed resulting in
  defect leakage.
- *Go to market of newer features/products were mostly not deployed
  on schedule.*
- *Lack of collaboration between product owners and engineering
  teams led to confusion around requirements and deliverables.*

The challenges discussed here were actually symptoms to a deeper
problem. Though the overall development methodology was agile

in nature with focus on continuous customer value creation, the QA function was not developed and equipped enough in its approach and strategy to support the agile structure.

Solution

Though the QA processes were concrete, implementation was falling short due to lack of evolved QA structure and tools and ongoing reliance on old QA practices. To tackle this situation, some gradual changes were made to strengthen the core QA processes stronger. In association with the complete engineering team, the exit criteria were revised to bring in service level agreements not only at the user story level but also at the sprint and then at the release level. This resulted in bringing clear understanding across the board for minimum quality requirements before the release.

The next step was to bring in tools for better collaboration within QA team and also among the rest of the engineering team and stakeholders—next-generation test management tools were also evaluated along the way. The aim was to have clear link between stories, test cases, test suites, test data, software builds, automated tests, test execution, and automated test results.

In addition, the automation framework was carefully selected, keeping the future in view not only from technology standpoint but from approach standpoint as well. This allowed at one hand to make the tests easier to script and easier to comprehend (for nontechnical stakeholders) as well as enabled developers to use the tests more proactively and better integrate them with automated software build tools. The approach of test automation was not only to test functional black box test cases but also to go a level deeper and automate the services and integration points with the database to make a holistic and comprehensive test suite.

The QA function was split into two parts with the new evolved roles in comparison to the earlier testing roles: solution analyst and QA analyst. A solution analyst is the crossover between a business analyst and a traditional QA tester. This enabled and further strengthened the project owner's role acting as the link between the engineering team and the stakeholders through defined requirements and its criteria of done through concrete test cases. The second role of a QA analyst is an evolved role where the testing team wore multiple hats, from refining test suites to executing them and automating them at the same time to build a robust regression test suite. This at one hand made the QA role creative and at the same time helped in cutting down the manual efforts required in regressing testing, thus giving more productive time to QA for better collaboration with the rest of the engineering team.

Approach

In addition to the changes described in the solution mentioned earlier, the whole QA function was based on the following three pillars:

Comprehensive Test Automation   A modular approach was taken toward test automation that linked each test case of a story to its automated test case; all of this was managed through the test management tool. This ensured extensive test coverage. The tests suites were grouped in various ways (again through test management tool) to serve various purposes—smoke tests (build verification), on-demand particular module/feature tests, sanity tests, sprint tests, and full regression tests (sign-off tests). Also, a set of tests were developed for execution on production environment to enable quick production verification, as well as continuous production monitoring from a functionality perspective. A complete test architectural framework was developed that catered to the needs of all stakeholders. For example, the test NG framework enabled easy scripting for testers on selenium, easy to comprehend test cases for nontechnical stakeholders, ease of maintainability and scaling up, distributed/parallel test execution (through grid), and also covered compatibility tests.

Continuously Refining and Enhancing Test Suites   With integration of tests with test management tool (Zephyr), it was built into the process to mark each test case as automated (including test data). The completion of test automation was brought in as part of the exit criteria. The focus was on cutting down at least 50% of efforts in manual execution of tests developed, sprint over sprint. The focus of the available bandwidth was shifted to continuously updating the automated test cases and leveraging them in different suites based on priority of the test case. With this, even defects that did not have a corresponding test case were automated to make the test suites robust. The QA analysts continuously worked in close tandem with development teams to learn and understand new services that were developed and automated by them.

Aim for Continuous Integration and Delivery   With the changes in QA approach as well as the overall engineering team, the challenges described earlier were tackled to a large extent. But still the complexity of multiple components on the platform and their parallel development posed a challenge. To overcome this challenge, the client adopted DevOps methodology to further integrate on the operations and delivery side. To enable this, the deployment process was streamlined and elaborated automated build process, and build management tools were introduced. To further enable the engineering team, QA integrated the test suites required at various phases of deployment as scheduled jobs in the automated software build tool. This not only, at one hand, significantly reduced the manual QA need but at the same time started providing up front test results on build stability on any environment without any human dependency.

Client Benefits

The change in QA approach over the last 2 years not only highly increased the reliability and quality of the production deployments, but it also significantly helped in expediting the QA process, bringing in very short but effective QA cycles. This further led to quick and early detection of defects, thus resulting in faster deployments. The case mentioned earlier brought in more confidence in the QA function, helped the product get a quality facelift, and also boosted the team's morale and positioning as a whole.

As testers, it is exciting to see what the future beholds. But this is also the time to take stock of the trends and prepare ourselves to brace such changes, which is what we will discuss in the next two chapters.

Did You Know?

1. While we fear if independent testing will cease to exist in the world of DevOps and mobile app development, studies show that it is poised to grow at 9.5% year on year until 2018.[2]
2. The average shelf life of a mobile application is only 30 days. This is a strong indicator of the need to scale up the quality of applications that are developed.[3]

References

1. Stepanek, M. http://www.brainyquote.com/quotes/authors/m/mattie_stepanek.html.
2. Thongkham, C. 2014. https://crowdsourcedtesting.com/resources/recent-trends-software-testing/.
3. Vasylyna, N. 2013. http://blog.qatestlab.com/2013/01/18/the-importance-of-mobile-application-testing/.

6

ARE WE EMPOWERED FOR THE PRESENT AND READY FOR THE FUTURE AS A FRATERNITY?

All things are ready, if our mind be so.

—**William Shakespeare,** *Henry V*[1]

Readiness is a state of mind. Once the mind is ready to tackle a problem and solve it, all energy will flow from within. Imagine the collective power of the testing fraternity, if we all concede to the change needed and take the step forward to empower ourselves to accomplish the new role in quality. To be able to prepare ourselves for this changing present and impending future, we first need to understand a few existing open questions. As an industry, we may not be able to resolve these questions right away—for all you know there is not even going to be a right or wrong answer. However, it is important to be aware of these and understand what meets the needs of your industry and career growth and accordingly how to prepare in ensuring that we are ahead of the curve. What are such open questions?

Is Test Automation Becoming Mandatory?

Rather than seeing test automation as mandatory if we as testers understand the value test automation brings in, in the current times, we will appreciate the need for it better and start leveraging it on our own. That will be a true win for software quality, for our careers, and for the overall industry rather than forcefully having our managers thrust test automation on to us. Such a positive move from the fraternity is what we really need at this time. So, why has really automation become so important at this time? A study shows what respondents have to say with increased test automation—72% say there is better detection of defects, 70% appreciate it for better test control and transparency, 69% recognize the shorter test cycles, and 66% give it to better test costs. Whatever the kind of tester you are on the team, now is the time to consider taking on test automation in possible ways, whether it be for product quality or for process and productivity improvement, as this is going to make all the difference in software testing in the coming years. With more test automation, continuous testing and quality is made possible, the dependency on a given tester is going to be brought down, and testers can refocus their priorities to taking up bigger and better areas of work that call for their core testing expertise and mind-set. The good thing is that the test automation technology and tool landscape have become very open. Having an understanding of any one programming language and the core testing fundamentals and an experience of using one tool, one should be able to fairly and flexibly adapt to newer test automation solutions. In several cases, for instance, even in our company at QA InfoTech, we leverage traditional automation engineers to build test frameworks, after which nonprogramming test engineers are able to take on test automation by using behavior-driven test approaches. Such newer approaches empower the large testing community that may have been so far comfortable only with manual testing, to take on automation with ease and without any inhibitions. This is important in the coming years as we prepare ourselves for the future.

Will Manual Testing Cease to Exist?

This is a long-debated question. The focus keeps changing from one to another, but at the current time, we are fairly stabilized in our test engineering processes and their alignment with the development cycle that we can say with certainty that manual testing will not cease to exist. Manual testing will further be elevated to become a niche—a niche where the focus will be on newer testing techniques that primarily look at end-user expectations; additional coverage scenarios that are brought in, in an exploratory manner field; and in-house studies that look at nonfunctional test areas such as usability and accessibility. Manual testing will be increasingly left to the more experienced testers who are able to look beyond the core requirements in not just evaluating the current product but also offering suggestions on its potential future implementations. It will become a proactive test cycle that simultaneously brings in requirements for subsequent considerations. Entry- and midlevel engineers who are into manual testing today should understand this to get themselves ramped up on test automation, as clearly we will see more and more of automation, in the basic test layers in the coming years—whether this be automated build verification tests, sanity tests, regression tests, and so on. Also, while the knowledge of a programming language is a huge advantage in picking up test automation skills, the lack thereof doesn't necessarily restrict one from working on test automation. Today, there are ample test automation frameworks, tools, and utilities that enable amateur automation engineers and manual testers to step into the test automation space. This would be a good place to start with and gradually ramp up on a programming language that best meets the needs of the work that the tester is involved in. In addition to this, once a manual tester, you are always a manual tester in some sense. So even if you move to test automation, you will see this in positive light where you are able to automate scenarios to increase your productivity and coverage and be able to simultaneously free up some time for out-of-box manual testing. Also, areas such as bug bashes, session-and charter-based exploratory testing, and crowdsourced testing are all becoming very valuable in bringing in more test coverage—these are tasks that are best done manually. With the increasing focus on end users, competitive positioning, and shift left approach to engineering, manual testing will soon elevate itself to the niche that will coexist with test automation.

Do I Have to Be a Domain Expert?

The days where a tester could say, "I understand test strategy, planning, design and execution; give me any task and I would be able to take on the test effort," are far gone. Such a generic tester can still exist today but will not be able to thrive. He will merely survive. The domain knowledge of the industry that a tester works in is becoming increasingly important. The workflows specific to the domain, compliances, checklists, user expectations, and target market are all becoming important to understand, to tailor a custom test effort that can differentiate the product in the market place. Since the organization anyways has the domain expertise, it is not going to be difficult for the testing group to access the right resources, to ramp up on the domain knowledge. However, oftentimes the domain scope is very large and the domain experts may be too deep into the subject that they may not be able to get to the basics of the knowledge sessions. In such cases, the team can look at having an official training imparted for their group and also target some domain-specific conferences to attend as such forums have a mix of expertise levels for them to pick from. You may not need to become a domain expert, but being privy into the latest domain's core fundamentals and leveraging them as required in ensuring app quality is becoming inevitable—both for the tester's performance and the product's quality.

How Do I Stay Current and Look ahead to Give Myself an Advantage?[2]

Staying challenged at work in any discipline can be difficult day after day, and software testing is no exception. On one hand, testers have to keep their heads down while working on tight schedules and perfecting the quality of the product under test. But on the other, technology is advancing at a rapid pace, and testers have to ensure they are not lagging behind in their skills. Testers need to constantly strike a balance between these two demands to stay challenged.

PractiTest's extensive State of Testing 2015 survey talks about inputs directly received from modern testers. Based on the responses that came in, the study calls testers "social beings" who often depend on sources such as social media, books, online communities, conferences, magazines, and competitions to keep up with the changes in the testing world.

They are also adopting new practices besides the core scripted manual and automated testing techniques, including user simulations, paired testing, user-coordinated beta and crowd testing efforts, and bug hunts. These practices help them stay better connected with end users and learn more on the ground.

The tester's role has itself expanded beyond the usual day-to-day testing effort. Testers are now required to wear multiple hats and handle new responsibilities such as test deployments, customer training, and developing internal tools. The tester's role in DevOps is also changing due to the demands on continuous integration.

While the debate of whether a tester needs to learn to code continues, the ones who can understand the system internals and the domain of the product under test will definitely be seen as a cut above the rest. The need to innovate is being felt in all disciplines, including software testing.

While all of these opportunities are exciting, how are testers managing and embracing them amidst the time challenges they have? The smart testers are integrating these learning solutions into their daily testing responsibilities. The survey mentioned earlier also talks about a very high number of testers learning hands-on, on the job, and through peer mentoring, and a significant number are also teaching themselves through books and online communities. These practices of on-the-job learning and mentoring also indirectly help the testers grow their communication, leadership, and management skills, which are very valuable today as well.

Will a Tester Be Embraced and Accepted into the DevOps Fold?

Times are changing today. It is a given that there is a need for more collaboration among the members of a product development team to survive in the marketplace and maintain an identity of their own. Such collaboration yields outcome not just in the bonding of the team but also in the quality and competitiveness of the product that is released. While it is no rocket science to understand the need for such collaboration, the true challenge is in implementing such a model especially between the testers and the rest of the product team, in an objective manner that is a win:win for everyone involved.

Obviously, the tester is no longer involved in merely executing test cases and reporting results. He has moved upstream, along with the test processes, where he is involved right from the product design stages. For instance, application performance considerations are being discussed up front and built in rather than being merely benchmarked and tuned later on. And the tester plays a critical role in such discussions, bridging the gap that long existed between development and quality.

While it is the tester's neck that is still out in the line if quality issues are found in production, the product team at large understands the role they play in contributing to a quality release. This is a welcome change and the tester is now transitioning into a role where he is empowering the rest of the team's own quality in possible ways—whether it be helping the developer build unit tests that are traceable to product requirements, enabling the build engineer and developer leverage a powerful set of automated tests for quick sanity tests, etc. All of these create a great opportunity to bond in the team, but if not handled well can also become a breeding ground for strained relations. One may see the other as trespassing into their scope of operations, taking undue charge of their team members, all of which can adversely impact the morale of the team and the quality of the product under development.

So, here is a situation where we understand the benefits if implemented but also the challenges in doing so—who is responsible in resolving this and embracing the testers effectively into the DevOps fold in this new role? This is a combined role of both the testers and the rest of the product team.

Let's start first with the rest of the team. It is certainly a mind shift where they now need to understand what the tester's new role is all about and why such a change is important in today's world of continuous integration. It is also equally important to understand this at an objective level to ensure there is no resentment or question of insecurity about one's own positioning in the team, given this new role of testers. Oftentimes, such doubts linger not just among the more junior members in the team but even among seniors and the more experienced. It is important to ease such questions and put to rest any such insecurities sooner than later to promote the right level of collaboration in the team. This is best done by senior management and could be done in forums such as "all-hands meetings" among other agenda items to explain the changing role of a discipline at large. This further needs to be followed up by smaller and more focused meetings among individual teams either at a product or a feature level, where questions and concerns if any can be addressed. The product development team should by now be at least partially ready to accept the testing team in their new avatar to enable DevOps.

While the preceding discussions start off the implementation on the right note, a lot has to do with how the testers take it along from this point on. They need to understand the true meaning of empowerment rather than seeing it as a right conferred on them. They need to amicably work with the teams to help them understand the true meaning of quality and what they can do to contribute. Along the way, they can bring in some fun factor through practices such as a weekly or monthly exploratory testing exercises and bug bashes, which will also help the rest of the team understand testing practices and management systems in an effective manner. It is important for the testers to showcase what other new tasks they are taking on, on their plate—whether it be interacting with end users, focusing on building quality not just in areas of defined requirements but also in areas of end-user expectations, evaluating quality of the product in line with competition in the market, looking for more optimization in test efforts, enhancing levels of test automation, etc. It is also in the knack and savviness of the tester to work cohesively with the product team in enabling quality, additionally leveraging the tools he has wherever possible. The question that often restrains these from happening is, "What if I don't get credit and recognition for what I have done?" Herein, I am not asking team members to give up on their career progression goals; once you understand that it takes two people to either make or break the relationship and apply this in a constructive manner to truly collaborate, it is not just one individual's career, but the entire team's progression that will get a positive facelift. All of this collaboration certainly calls for free flowing knowledge, sharing of tools and frameworks, ease in accessing people whenever needed, and a true belief in the model of teamwork. When this happens, even issues, if any, can be mutually resolved in a mature manner, thereby truly accepting a tester into the DevOps fold.

Is Independent Testing Dying?

Amidst all of this buzz for upstream quality, increased collaboration among team members, freelance app/mobile development, and collective ownership for quality, while it is exciting to see more people partake in contributing to a quality release, the underlying concern that cannot be ignored is whether independent testing is withering away. As testers, it has taken us a long time to establish the status of independence in testing—a status where there is unbiased test coverage and evaluation done by a group of people who have not been involved in product development, at least in the given release. ISTQB calls independence a range rather than a condition, swaying all the way on the spectrum from "no independence" to "full independence":

1. At one end of the spectrum, the absence of independence is where all testing is done by the programmer.
2. Moving along, we have integrated testers—who closely collaborate with developers and report into the same development manager.
3. Further along, you have testers working outside of but with development and reporting to the same project management office.
4. At the extreme end, you have full independence, where testers report to a completely independent business head.

All along these four range positions, outsourced test vendors can really fit in anywhere in the spectrum. When independent testing first evolved in the late 1990s, testers moved from state 1 to state 4 directly in this spectrum. Now, we are gradually moving inward into states 3 and 2, which is why the fear on whether we will or we have lost our independence. Undoubtedly, there are organizations that have a merged role of developers and testers, where people assume cross functions. So, is independence really lost in such cases? With due care and execution from the testing fraternity and sensitization of the product team, independence can be retained and resurrected in these challenging times. This is going to be very important for the coming years as software development landscape changes significantly. Let's see how.

Independence Need Not Come in Just from Testers

We often think the independence factor comes in only from the testers, whereas in essence it can come in from anyone who has not directly worked on coding the module under test. It could thus be designers, build engineers, business and marketing team members, external team developers, end users, crowd users who are testers, users or domain experts, etc. When such a strong independent team is put together in addition to the core additional test team, the unbiased evaluation is able to cover new scenarios, in shorter time and lesser cost. Freelance developers also need to understand this, as studies show that the average shelf life of a mobile application is only 30 days. Given the time and effort that goes in such development, you would agree that is a dangerously low number. If this has to be improved, independent and unbiased testing is important. Also, even in teams where there are no testers, at least a round robin style of development can be adopted where one may be a developer in the current release but a tester in the next and so on.

Understand the Dotted Line in Role Delineation between Developers and Testers[3]

A couple of years back, one of our employees had written an article for a leading software test publication on this topic. While collaboration between testers and the rest of the team is inevitable and valuable in its own ways, it is important to tread the thin line of distinction between developers and testers very carefully, failing which there is a good chance of team morale issues, impacted product quality, role trespass, etc. It is thus important to identify areas where such sensitivity and role ambiguity exist and play carefully. For example, a tester may sometimes be required to suggest solutions for the defects filed—herein, he may be expected to make some small changes especially in content files for locale fixes. Similarly, he may be required to help the developers identify unit test scenarios, take on static code reviews, etc. Likewise, developers who are using the test automation suite may notice areas of improvement to work on. All of these are sensitive touch points where the entities should be careful to ensure they do only the bare minimum that is required. Anything over and above will dilute their focus and waste their time and may also create insecurities among team members.

Understand What Role a Tester Should Assume at This Time

As part of maintaining independence, if testers understand their core role and the add-ons that will help bring in value, we can be rest assured that the independence can be preserved for the immediate present and into the future. Herein, the tester has to appreciate the need and importance of test automation, understand where manual tasks come in handy (especially in cases of nonfunctional testing such as performance, security, usability, and accessibility), and test centers of excellence and how each of these will help them tie in their efforts to the overall product quality goals.

With care taken on these fronts, independent testing is here to stay and for the right reasons to uphold product quality and the tester's career.

Other Additional Best Practices to Adopt to Empower Ourselves for the Present and Prepare for the Future

Stay Hungry, Foolish, and Continuously Challenged

This is an adage that became very popular when Steve Jobs quoted it in one of his last public speeches. In today's world, amidst the constraints we work within, staying hungry and foolish is even more important. It can help you stay challenged in your testing career for advancing in your professional and personal growth. Given how dynamic the technology landscape is, the ongoing culture of learning and staying challenged is what will make all the difference in the coming years.

Adopt Continuous Improvement

A mere desire to learn and not knowing how to go about with it will not get the tester very far. In the self-managed teams that we are working in today, the tester needs to devise his own plans to embrace continuous improvement. The best way to achieve this would be to regularly introspect test processes; evaluate how other teams are working; keep tabs on latest in the industry through new feeds, forums, and conferences; and evaluate which would make sense for him and the team. While this is connected in one way to the earlier point, this is more focused on an actionable set of practices rather than the desire to stay hungry.

Work Is Not Just a 9–5 Job

As we further empower ourselves for the coming years, it is important to really get out of the 9–5 working day mind-set. Granted, in the IT industry, this does not happen very often and we are typically working long hours, taking calls and accessing e-mails from home, etc. However, this point is more than such out of office premises hours that we clock in. Quality has to be ingrained in the tester's mind—today's test scenarios are all around us; users are all around us. You could, for instance, take a cab ride to the airport and how the driver uses specific mobile applications may give you ideas for your own application. News items—what you hear, see, and read—can give you ideas. Stay curious and work on connecting external events to internal processes, practices, and scenarios.

1. *Think customizations*: Quality is increasingly becoming a customized function. Software development itself has become a very customized area of work. While organizations want to learn from industry best practices and adopt trends, they understand the value of customizations. For example, a survey shows 92% of the respondents leveraging agile development practices. But these are all not "one size fits all" adoption. A lot of customization is taken up to align with the organization's requirements, user needs, specific market parameters, domain under consideration, etc. As a tester, similarly, it is becoming increasingly important to think customizations, whether it be in testing processes, tools, or frameworks to ensure you are effective and productive on an ongoing basis.

2. *Be ever ready*: Whether it is a one-day pass, one-hour pass, a customer interaction, or a partner collaboration, testers will have to increasingly be ever ready on the job. It is also not just about being instructed on what needs to be done. As testers, we need to be ever ready to consume things around us and see how they can be translated into actionable items to improve what we do and the quality of the product under test. Such diligence, watchfulness, and attention to detail will differentiate the best testers from the rest and also prepare the fraternity as a whole for the coming years.

As we question our empowerment for the present and readiness for the future, a key thing to remember is that all of this readiness is not necessarily sought externally. A tester has to internally look for and prepare himself too, as a lot depends on the tester's mental readiness and subsequent efforts to align with the required change.

Did You Know?[4,5]

1. The current spend on quality as a percent on the IT budget is 36. This is expected to reach 40 by 2018.
2. Ten percent of the surveyed respondents state that they plan to build Agile test centers of excellence in the coming 2 years.
3. Over two million mobile applications are available in app stores as of November 2015.
4. Global testing services market is expected to grow at about 11% between 2013 and 2018.
5. Of the tasks that testers are taking up in addition to test execution, the most significant one is that of managing testing and development environments. Sixty-three percent have said to be taking this task up.
6. Exploratory session-based testing is a new technique that several testers are increasingly leveraging. About 85% of the respondents have said to be using this.

References

1. Shakespeare, W. *Henry V.* http://www.goodreads.com/quotes/tag/readiness.
2. Padmanaban, R. 2015. https://www.techwell.com/techwell-insights/2015/07/how-stay-challenged-your-testing-career.
3. Padmanaban, R. 2013. http://www.stickyminds.com/article/dotted-line-role-delineation-between-developer-and-tester.
4. http://www.pocketgamer.biz/metrics/app-store/app-count/.
5. CapGemini. Annual report. https://www.capgemini.com/thought-leadership/world-quality-report-2015-16.

7

HOW IS THE TESTER'S ROLE CHANGING?

It is not the strongest or the most intelligent who will survive but those who can best manage change.

—**Charles Darwin**[1]

Over the course of this book, we have already seen that change is inevitable. The technologies we work with, the products we build, the users we cater to, their requirements, our processes, and the roles testers play—literally everything changes over the course of time. One thing that is constant is the fact that change is inevitable. Going by this mantra, the tester's role has also been subjected to a lot of change in the recent times. Understanding the need for the change, the exact change, its impact, and how one should align himself with the call of the hour are all very important in ensuring positive outcomes. In this chapter, we will probe into how exactly the tester's role has changed in the recent years and what to expect in the coming years.

The core of what we do as a tester has not really changed much—for instance, it is still and will continue to be important for us to understand that the product should be tested for its functionality, user interface, usability, performance, security, and interoperability, etc. These attributes that validate and verify a product continue to be time tested and proven. The role of a tester is rather changing in the way he tests for these attributes, how he gets the job done, how he interacts with the rest of the team, how the team perceives what a tester does, and his strategy on how to achieve quality within the constraints that he operates within. So, what are those core points on which the tester's new role is being defined?

Become a quality leader, advocate, and practitioner: A tester is a quality practitioner to start with. He plays an active role in finalizing the test strategy, determining the entry and exit criteria, and determining what test execution methods to adopt in effectively delivering a quality product. In his new role though, he is more of a quality advocate. He is actively getting the rest of the team onboard with this thought process on quality, enabling them to adopt quality practices too. The rest of the team is looking up to the tester to understand what it takes to building a quality product. It is not a new phenomenon where the tester is stepping up to being a quality leader and advocate, helping the rest of the team to embrace quality. What is new though is that he does it in a level-headed capacity, not trespassing any other product team member's area of work. The tester now understands that it is in the best interest of the product and associated elements of schedule and cost to ensure quality is taken up from the inception stages of product development. A true tester is the one that engages himself from the early stages to help others own quality, evaluates the changing facets of quality for his own product, and aligns his execution strategies with such changing needs. He is thus a true leader, advocate, and practitioner for quality.

Question one's capabilities for ongoing continuous improvement: A tester's role today is certainly at a complex crossroad. The user expectations are changing, test matrices are expanding, timelines are shrinking, and budgets are being cut—all of which are forcing the tester to reinvent himself. Some of the veterans of the software testing industry formulated a course on rapid software testing, to address exactly this scenario. What if someone were to give you just an hour to test a product—while everyone understands it as an impossible feat to accomplish—how smart a tester you are in optimizing the resources available on hand to achieve the best possible coverage. This is increasingly becoming the need of the day and is covered well in topics such as rapid software testing.[2] As a tester, it is absolutely important to constantly question one's skill set and see whether they are up to date with the need of the hour and if not seek opportunities to bring in ongoing continuous improvement. Today's tester needs to resell himself—we are at a stage where on one hand, testers are stepped up to be quality leaders, while on the other, their role is questioned in some cases. The tester has to be able to speak up for himself, explain what his role exactly is, and what would happen if he did not exist. The list that I outline in the following will help him do this and in some sense also help him chalk his own role depending on the needs of his organization and product:

1. Representative of end user on the product team, translating their requirements into suggestions and enhancements to build into the product.
2. True evaluator of competitor offerings in comparison with richness of one's own solution.
3. Automation enabler (whether he does the automation himself or is taken up by someone else such as developer) to bring in repeatability, consistency, and precision into the quality process.
4. Strategy designer and implementer to align the quality goals with other business goals in true belief that quality is an important and inevitable ingredient in the mix to a successful market launch.
5. Constructive destructor to catch as many issues as possible before the user notices them.
6. Enabler to quickly and effectively fix issues caught both in testing and live environments and help the team understand the user impact of reported issues to ascertain the defect fix priorities.
7. Optimizer that balances varied testing scenarios against available time and budget to maximize test coverage.
8. Help the team understand the quality risks associated with the changes they make, in an Agile environment.
9. Collaborate with the programmer to catch issues as they get into the product, rather than catching them days later, in the current compressed development cycles.
10. An unbiased entity that can bring in conscious, collaborative, and continuous quality into the product under test.
11. Explain that collaboration with developer will happen—you will understand system internals and contribute to a quality development effort, but why your unbiased test cycles are important for the larger emphasis on continuous quality.

Savvy team member: The tester has always been the one with most touch points for communication in the product team. Now, with a role where a tester is a quality advocate on the team, he needs to be increasingly savvy in his role. He will have to deal with a lot of sensitivities, along the way, as he helps his team members own quality. Herein, a tester's role calls for maturity to be able to handle all team members in a savvy manner, not losing focus of the larger quality goal. Especially in areas where he walks a thin line, such as the role delineation between a developer and a tester,[3] there is room for conflicts if the situation is not managed well. The tester has an important role to play to empower team bonding.

At QA InfoTech, we publish a quarterly magazine dedicated to quality. We have external contributors also sharing their thoughts herein on latest and greatest in quality. In a recent edition, we had a quality leader Rahul Vishwaroop from Adobe to share his insights on what 2016 may look like for a tester. For more details, this is available in Chapter 8—but to summarize them at a high level in this chapter, he talks about the role of a tester where it is important to understand the touch devices and testing for the same, mobile first testing, proactive feedback seeking from social platforms, agility in release cycles, compressed endgame certification, connected workflows, and the role of security to realign a tester's role in today's world.

As a tester works on his skills to be a savvy team member, it is important to understand he will also have to part with some of his tasks on hand and be ready to take on new tasks. A give-and-take approach thus becomes important. One of my work colleagues did a keynote on this topic in STC 2013 (a leading testing conference in India) on *The New Gives and Takes in a Software Tester's Role*. This was very well received and the full presentation is available online.[4] The crux of this message is about how a tester today has to increasingly revisit his role on a more frequent basis to give away tasks that don't make any more business sense in the current day and instead take on tasks that are more relevant. Also, some of these are tasks that the team gives away completely, while some are tasks that you swap with another member of the product team. The presentation talks about how to give away the following in totality from a tester's plate:

1. *Detailed documentation and test artifact creation*: With the Agile wave in full swing, a common misconception people have is documentation should be completely given up.

Documentation is indeed important, but what to cut down on is what one needs to look at. For example, "Do we need to have detailed test strategies that are often not referred to later on?" and "Do we need to create detailed step-by-step tests?" are all questions testers need to ask themselves. This is also the place where smart processes can be adopted. For example, technologies such as augmented reality can be leveraged to make a tester's life simpler and more productive. It can help process test results and log them in test case management tools saving time for the tester. We did a webinar for Eurostar in 2015, talking about how augmented reality can be useful to improve a tester's efficiency. The full recording of the session is available at https://testhuddle.com/resource/the-connect-between-augmented-reality-and-software-testing.[5]

2. *Pure script-based testing approach*: This includes both manual and automated test scripts. The basic idea here is that once a tester hooks himself to just script-based testing, his out-of-box thinking and creativity soon recedes. The combination of a scripted approach and a free flow or guided exploratory testing effort is definitely well worth and is indeed the right balance that testers need to work toward.

3. *Obsession on age-old test metrics that don't add any value*: In some cases today, even numbers such as return on investment on test automation are being questioned. Metrics have long helped bring in objectivity into a test effort. However, what gets often forgotten is that metrics age over time (sometimes even in short windows) and will need to be periodically revisited for their worth and updated as needed. Sticking on to age-old metrics is more of an overhead than any value they bring in.

What Can a Tester Give away to Another Team Member?

1. Build verification test execution can be handed off to a developer.
2. Sanity test suites can again be handed off to the developer, to help take up periodic quality checks and verify bug fixes effectively.

3. Early troubleshooting tests to the operations and support team, to handle field issues with a faster turnaround.

4. Accountability for quality to everyone on the team to step into a more advocating and practitioning role.

This list outlines an easy set of tasks that the tester can give away to another member, not necessarily to create more bandwidth on his plate, but to help everyone own quality better. For example, handing off the build verification tests to the developer will enhance the chances of getting a good build to test, sooner, than if the tester took on these tests himself. Also, giving these away to another person on the product team does not mean the tester washes off his responsibilities. He is still responsible to enable them use these tests effectively, help resolve any queries they may have, maintain the tests on a periodic basis, etc., to empower them derive the true value of handling these test suites.

What Can a Tester Take on His Plate Instead?

At the end of the day, it is all a give and take. If the tester had shed off so much from his plate, what can he take on, in line with the needs of the current testing discipline? He should certainly explore to take on bigger and better things, including more extrinsic focused testing, such as more end-user analysis and competitive analysis to bring in more expectation-driven requirements that are built into the product up front.

1. Ownership to building a professional culture for quality
2. Controlled freedom with responsibility
3. Competing product quality evaluation
4. Triage representation
5. End-user issue analysis
6. Role of quality consultant/ambassador

While these points are easier prescribed than followed, it is important for the team at large, including the management, to understand the importance of this changing role in the new times. They will have to step in to ensure they are implemented well and customized to the needs of the organization. If they do not step in, a lot of anxiety, insecurity, and resentment among the product team will prevail, which will further adversely impact team morale.

A Fluid Role

The word "fluid" or "dynamic" probably best describes the change in the role of a tester. A tester has to be as dynamic as possible today in shaping his role on the go. In conferences that I have been to, the task that is often asked is to clearly list out a tester's role. I don't think there is a concrete answer to this, as this changes depending on the organization, product, and user base that the tester is dealing with. At a high level, we can say the tester's role is to enable product quality, strategize, and implement tests to inject quality into the product from the early stages and represent the end users in engineering both system requirements and user expectations into the product under test. He should take on all these, with best possible collaboration with the rest of the team, and objectivity through the use of metrics and service-level agreements, to bring in continuous and conscious quality. However, what is becoming important is an element of context. Given the global product base, context-driven testers are very important. These are testers that are aware of the market requirements of the product, the sensitivities of the global markets, and the compliances that are important to adhere to (be it domain based, geography based, or attribute based) and accordingly bring in a mix of scripted and unscripted test scenarios to work within the time and cost constraints on hand. Such testers are increasingly becoming indispensable, and to be able to achieve such a contextual and creative state, the tester has to mold his role to be fluid enough. He should be able to chalk his role himself under the guidance of his team and managers rather than wait to be told what his role needs to be.

Changing Facets in Software Quality That Will Additionally Define a Tester's Role in the Coming Years

1. *Need to resurrect the core value of independent testing*: I had discussed this in detail in the previous chapter on whether we are ready to handle the changes as a fraternity. The understanding as to why conscious independent quality is important, along with how to collaborate to bring in productivity and efficiency in operations, will together define a tester's role moving forward. This is precisely why testers need to resell themselves as discussed earlier.

2. *Automation testing will become mainstream*: Automation will play a very important role moving forward in assuring quality. Today, automation is very feasible even for nonprogrammers. Test frameworks enable behavior- and context-driven automation, which are easily understood and implemented by one and all. While some very seasoned and mature testers can still thrive without being involved in test automation, the bulk of us will have to train in this area to redefine our role moving forward.

3. *Manual testing will become a niche*: This is again an area we discussed at length in the previous chapter. To reiterate here, a tester needs to redefine his role with the right balance of manual and automated testing to bring in the required quality coverage in the available time and cost on hand. Manual testing will lean more toward exploratory and out-of-box test scenarios in the coming years, while the more predictable ones will be candidates for test automation, among other variables to consider.

4. *Mobile first initiative*: This will increasingly play an important role in the tester's profile and tasks. Mobile first is a global initiative today with leading app makers looking to offer app-only solutions. The way we test on a mobile device is quite different—while the scenarios may be in common, the tools we use and the matrix we choose are all drastically different. The testers of today's generation (those that have less than 5 years of experience) are more exposed to mobile computing and scenarios and have a better mind-set alignment to mobile testing, whereas those of us with longer testing experience have to unlearn and relearn a few concepts to train to think along mobile testing. This will play an important part in defining a tester's role in the coming years.

A Constant Innovator

A tester in his new role needs to be a constant innovator. He is someone who is always looking to enhance test processes, product quality, team bonding, collective thinking, embracing new technologies, etc. A tester who incorporates these in his role today will be better able to differentiate himself from the rest, in the coming times. QA InfoTech's evangelist spoke about this at a keynote in a leading test conference in India in 2014. The full session is available here[6]—https://www.youtube.com/watch?v=Yik-G83d9l8—for your reference.

As we wrap up this chapter on the changing role of a software tester, I want to leave you all with an interesting and relevant story that truly sums the message I want you all to think about.

It is the famous hare and tortoise story that we all have heard as kids, where the hare and the tortoise decide to race. The hare is complacent and overconfident about his running skills and loses to the tortoise because he becomes lazy. The moral is *slow and steady wins the race.*

There are three other sequels to this story that fit very aptly to our needs here. In sequel two, the hare does some soul searching and finds out why he lost the race, so he invites the tortoise to race again. He is fast and steady this time, winning the race hands down. Our takeaway here is "slow and steady is good, but fast and steady is even better." So, someone who is faster and equally consistent in an organization will be able to shine better than the others.

In the third sequel to this story, the tortoise does his soul searching. He knows what his capabilities are and tries to see if there is a way for him to win. He finds new playing fields that are dynamic and provide better potential for him to excel. So, he invites the hare to the race again, incorporating a river along the racetrack this time. The hare is fast in this race too, until he reaches the river. He freezes, not knowing how to proceed, while the slow and steady tortoise gets there and swims his way to the finishing line. The moral of this sequel is "identify and leverage core competencies and explore new playing fields for growth and advancement."

In the final sequel, by which time the hare and tortoise have become good buddies, the two decide to run together to the finish line as a team. They understand that doing this together will be more fun, effective, and successful for both of them. So, the tortoise jumps on the hare's back to get all the way to the river. At that point, the hare jumps on the tortoise's back to cross the river and reach the finish line. This is the sequel testers need to understand and buy into, the moral here being "teamwork is about situational leadership and empowerment." The person with relevant core competency in a situation should take the lead so the group can shine together. A give-and-take approach lets the team win together with much less overall effort but much more fun and collaboration. This approach also adds the elements of fluidity, continuous learning, savviness and collective effort, and situational leadership, all of which shape a tester's role to success and enhance the acceptance of a quality product in the marketplace.

At the end of the day, quoting Shakespeare, it is not in the stars that holds our destiny, but in ourselves. Let's take control of such destiny, be cognizant of the changes required in the current times, and ride the wave smooth and high to emerge as successful testers and hold up our profession's brand.

Did You Know?

1. The starting salary for a software tester could be in the $20 an hour ballpark, with the experienced easily making over $85,000 a year.[7]
2. Myths continue to haunt a software tester's role around the job description, job role, pay, etc. The industry is however beginning to differentiate and discard such myths from facts.[8]
3. While we have discussed varied skills to succeed as a software tester over the course of this book, if you were to look at the top few, it is a mix of both hard/technical and soft skills. At the end of the day, a mix of these are important and you cannot isolate one from the other.[9]

References

1. Kerpen, D. http://www.inc.com/dave-kerpen/11-powerful-quotes-to-inspire-your-team-to-embrace-change.html.
2. Bach, J. 2013. http://www.satisfice.com/videos.shtml.
3. Padmanaban, R. 2013. http://www.stickyminds.com/article/dotted-line-role-delineation-between-developer-and-tester.
4. QA InfoTech. 2013. The new gives and takes in a tester's role. https://www.youtube.com/watch?v=uoaP-0apQ10.
5. Test Huddle admin. 2015. Testing in the augmented reality world. https://testhuddle.com/resource/the-connect-between-augmented-reality-and-software-testing/.
6. QA InfoTech. 2014. Five quick bites to innovate in software testing. https://www.youtube.com/watch?v=Yik-G83d9l8.

7. http://www.jobs.net/Article/CB-58-Talent-Network-IT-A-Close-Look-9-Facts-About-Software-Testers/.

8. Admin. 2016. http://www.softwaretestinghelp.com/is-software-testers-job-really-low-profile-job/.

9. Admin. 2016. http://www.softwaretestinghelp.com/top-5-things-tester-must-have-to-excel/.

8

WHAT DO INDUSTRY VETERANS HAVE TO SAY?

A mentor empowers a person to see a possible future, and believe it can be obtained.

—**Shawn Hitchcock**

This quote reflects the sentiment with which I reached out to a few industry veterans to get their thoughts on where quality is heading in the larger IT scenario, in the coming years. Such veterans help us see what is coming and also guide us into preparing for it, not because as individual testers we are not capable of setting our own direction, but because most often, such directional guidance is important to bring in clarity among randomization, chaos, and complex dynamics.

I have inputs from three senior people in the industry, two from the United States and one from India, who have graciously shared their inputs for this effort with their take on where software quality is heading and what is in store.

Tom Churchwell's Input[1]

A career as a military pilot, with a parallel career in IT, has been an eclectic backdrop to Tom's professional world. With leadership roles in banking, aerospace, and healthcare, Tom has consulted for Fortune 1000 companies throughout Michigan and been a part of organizational transformation in a wide variety of cultures and environments. He gets jazzed helping teams transition toward more self-organization, continuous improvement, and higher performance. Tom enjoys learning, people, and the challenges associated with creating outstanding competitive differentiation.

Tom's Thoughts on Future of Quality and Software Testing

There is an explosion of growth in technologies and the impact on all of us has been profound. Since the moment we started connecting everyone, everywhere, to everything, our little rock in the universe, or at least the people on it, shot off in a new and exciting direction. We now have access to all of the knowledge of human history, literally, at our fingertips, and if you look around, you can see almost everyone is absorbed with that little supercomputer we now carry with us 24/7. We have come a long way from the days of punch cards and to quote Jerry Garcia, "What a long strange trip it has been."

Between social media and ubiquitous Internet access, we can do things now that most of us, even a decade ago, never imagined. There is no need to go "Back to the Future" because the future is now. As we find more we are able to do, the window just keeps opening to all of the things we still want to be able to do. For good or for ill, we have truly entered a "Brave New World." We have a plethora of apps to choose from, and we are a fickle bunch. We want to be able to do almost anything, with the touch of a finger. We want both high quality and high performance and we have the ability to search for the people and products who can give us what we demand. Customer expectations for speed, quality, and usability are at an all-time high and if we don't like something, we have ways to let everyone know about it.

Quality, like performance, is like a multifaceted diamond; when you look at it from different angles, something else catches your eye. Similarly, the dimensions of quality testing seem to keep growing with new devices, tools, technologies, and methodologies. Agile development has been putting testing first, likely where it should have been all along, but more than that, it has introduced a sea change to the importance of teamwork and automation. Whether your organization has dipped its toe in the agile waters or not, the effect it has had on tools, practices, and expectations cannot be ignored. Quality professionals are striving to keep abreast of these changes and prepare for the changing expectations they represent.

I used to be a programmer for an aerospace company, and at the time, I was also a pilot. We built flight simulators and whenever we had a release that needed to be tested, naturally, they would ask me to "fly the sim" and check it out. Being technical, I did a multitude of other testing as well. Over time, we got more contracts for more different aircraft types and I ended up spending more time flying/testing than I did programming. I really looked forward to my job each day and ended up spending several years with that company.

Working in aerospace had many advantages, one of which was the top tier talent I got to work with. I loved programming, and it seemed like there was always something new to learn. My experience coding has served me well as a tester, particularly when I look back at how the industry has been changing over the past decade. When I first started testing, we did almost everything manually. We poured over thick requirements documents to glean test and acceptance criteria and then compiled every step for everything we were going to test ahead of time into spreadsheets that we used over and over. It was laborious and sometimes tedious and so very important!

The pace of change has not abated, and there is still always something new to learn. Automated testing and the skill of coding are becoming critical to being a successful QA professional. With the advent of agile, testers are becoming an integral part of a cross-functional delivery team. They are no longer separated from programmers, but rather sit side by side helping increase the velocity of the whole team by testing early and often and sometimes even hold onto your hat pairing up to do some coding.

In this new environment, new skills are needed. Collaboration and coordination skills are as important, maybe even more important, than they ever were. Trust with customers, with team members, between teams, and between individuals is like a marker for success. If you don't have it, you will most likely fail. If you do have it, it may be invisible to an outsider, but it is the hard won differentiator that will help your team succeed when the going gets tough. Trust, when you have it, translates into the ability to, as a team, overcome obstacles that would otherwise stymie the team and stall the project.

In the old days, QA testers spent a lot of time alone, doing all of the testing. Nowadays, the most important QA skill needed is rooted in teamwork and the ability to manage commitments. QA professionals need the ability to ensure all of the right testing gets done and done right, whether by them or the rest of the team. This incredible change, in both the perception of the role of QA and the skills needed to be successful in that role, is just a single example of the changes occurring for QA professionals. Our world, industry, and organizations keep changing and we cannot afford to be left behind. Nobody has a crystal ball, or at least not one that works, and so knowing what will succeed and what will become obsolete is hard to predict. I feel almost queasy at the thought of trying to predict the future; if I were any good at it, I would be gambling all of my money in Las Vegas or other people's money on Wall Street and I do neither of those. Even so, there are trends in the industry we can look to.

The "Ante" for Products

Every industry has standards, best practices, minimum viable launch criteria, or whatever you want to call the "ante" to just get in the game. These are the "whats" of software testing.

Software needs to be

- Reliable—Does what is expected, when expected
- Responsive—Got to be fast
- Available—From just about any device, from just about any-where, in just about any language, even if I am disabled in some way
- Maintainable—Needs to be built for change because the world is not standing still
- Secure—Both my device(s) and my data

This is an important list, but not in any particular order.

The plethora of tools and practices that allow us to meet the minimum expectations of our users and of industry is exploding and that trajectory will likely continue into at least the near future. For example, testing automation has permeated every aspect of functionality. From the user interface to APIs and business logic, from accessibility and usability to performance, and from services layers to deeper levels of unit testing, automation has become an integral part of the architecture and delivery process. In some organizations, builds and releases are being automated to create an ability to deliver software in a continuous steady stream just as fast and programmers can churn it out. In fact, for those continuous delivery organizations, full-stack automation is the backbone that makes it all work.

The Cloud, the Crowd, and Distributed Teams

And then there is "The Cloud." The trend towards commoditized technologies has leveled the playing field such that start-ups can compete with the largest international conglomerates; a brave new world indeed. The glass windows of the isolated data center have all been smashed. The special access of the "Super User" is available to everyone now. A lot of the skills of the SysAdmin have been abstracted into a relatively user friendly AWS interface. Almost anyone can build out a computer system with "virtually" unlimited scalability and speed. With Moore's Law still in effect, infrastructure technologies are becoming more abundant.

People and teams are all over the globe. Crowd funding and crowd testing are crowding the market. The cloud, crowd, and continuous delivery are as much about technologies as they are about collaboration, coordination, and effectiveness with people. The cloud may be the place to get things done, but the challenges of time zones, languages, norms, standards, and expectations impinge on the interpersonal trust levels that teams need to move at the pace of today's business. Teams need to quickly build trust and the ability to communicate, coordinate, and collaborate effectively across the globe. This presents challenges we've never had to face before.

Many of these trends are already well known, so what is new and different? Keeping up with technology is a bare minimum, but what, as a professional, should I concentrate on learning in order to stand out with my peers?

In the past, in general, teams worked in one geographical location. We found help from our trusted network of people with whom we had worked. The world and our projects are far more dynamic now. More often, we need to find unique specialists for our team who can be trusted to deliver and we may never even meet them face to face. We need new criteria for deciding with whom we want to work and our criteria need to include their trustworthiness as well as their technical prowess.

Bringing Quality Closer to the Customer

Quality expertise is needed at every phase of solution delivery (Figure 8.1). A bad rap on social media can kill a product before it

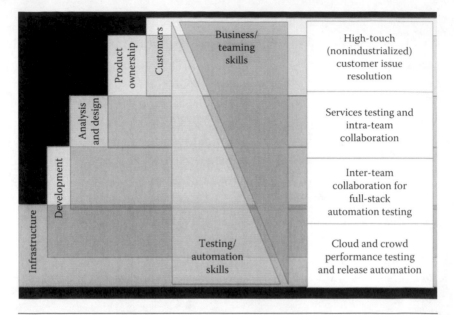

Figure 8.1   Bringing quality closer to the customer.

gets off the ground. High-touch, nonindustrialized, speedy customer issue resolution is a new competitive advantage and quality expertise is needed to make it work. Today's service-oriented architectures produce system interdependence that did not exist before. One changed or broken service can cause a domino effect breaking a multitude of other services unexpectedly. At the services layer, automated test suites that ensure new service functionality won't break other services is becoming mandatory as is the QA expertise to produce those test suites. In team rooms, developers and testers are becoming more distributed. The more diverse and the more dispersed the team, the more important the skill of coordinating their efforts.

The world and the markets are moving way too fast to have teams isolated from each other with bureaucracy and onerous processes. Streamlined delivery, with steady streams of updates, is not just anticipated, but expected. Rather than the exception, in the future, continuous delivery will be the norm. That means quality has to be addressed continuously too.

Quality is a fundamental part of what makes customers happy and so it needs to be assessed and addressed throughout development. Throw it over the wall for quality is a dead practice from the 1990s.

QA experts will no longer be sequestered as a separate part of the organization. Rather than try to test the quality in after all the development is done, teams need to bake quality in throughout the development. Now, QA testers are part of the development team from beginning to end.

The "Ante" for People

Radical change can also reveal rare opportunity. From a business perspective, "it" is more about helping a team innovate and produce competitive advantage; creating a safe and trusting environment where innovation can emerge. That is the "it" we need to get, and if you "get it," it will change what you concentrate on learning.

> Technologies are a means to an end; they come and go. Knowing great technologies will not help you fund your retirement or send your children to college, but the ability to build trust with teams, organizations, and customers will.

In times of radical change, then, there is an opportunity to stand out among peers as one "who gets it." The same way customers want products they can trust, we want teammates we can trust. Whether you are a garage start-up or an international conglomerate, you need people to bring your product to the market; trustworthy teams make it happen.

Hierarchies and a command-and-control approach are proving ineffective in the fast-moving dynamic world we are inheriting. Servant leaders, autonomous self-organizing teams, and craftsmanship are proving to be competitive differentiators. The skill to elicit effective promises, and deliver on promises of our own, is at the root of building products that teams are proud of. Those teams produce products that gain customer loyalty. Team dynamics matter because if we fail to meet our commitments to each other as a team, our products will likely fail to meet the expectations of our customers.

These skills of coordination, collaboration, and effective execution are even more important as our teams become more distributed.

In the fast-paced, dynamic world we have inherited, the tools for effective execution are not detailed project plans or detailed requirements. Teams need the ability to dance with the change: pivot or persevere depending on feedback from customers, product owners, and teammates. It is the small stuff, rigorous promise-keeping; clarifying what is expected, when, and how—that makes the difference.

At the end of the day, nobody has a reliable crystal ball, but there are trends we can expect to see continue. Technologies will continue to evolve and teams will continue to need clearings created for them to perform at a high level. The demands of the market to make it better, faster, and easier to use will continue. In the short term, the cloud, crowd, and continuous delivery will be touch points of massive change. QA professionals need to learn these technologies and help their teams adopt them. Quality will continue to be an essential part of every team and product, and full-stack automation testing will grow in importance. Smaller, faster, more nimble, and more autonomous teams will succeed more often than the monolithic, process-heavy, segregated teams of the past. Teams will continue to become more agile as will their organizations.

The skills needed to succeed in this new reality will be much different than before. Teamwork, courageous collaboration, mind-set for openness and discovery, and the passion for lifelong learning will become more important as the world continues to change. The market for people will become more dynamic and so is the art of finding people with the right skills and who share your passions and want to be part of your team—is becoming an essential skill for leaders. It really is impossible to predict the future, but there is one thing we can be fairly confident about. The increasing pace of change will continue increasing and dealing with that is going to be our greatest challenge.

Ross Smith's Input[2]

Ross is a Director of Engineering at Microsoft for the Skype customer experience team. He is a fellow of the Royal Society for the Encouragement of Arts, Manufactures, and Commerce, which aims to enrich society through ideas and action. Ross is an author of The Practical Guide to Defect Prevention *and holder of six patents. He developed 42Projects, which focuses on management innovation, trust, and the application of games at work. A frequent speaker at the Serious Games Summit and Gamification Summit, Ross works with teams inside and outside Microsoft on deploying games in the workplace.*

Ross's Inputs on Where We Are Heading

I first started writing code in 1978. I was fortunate to have a high school math class with an HP teletype machine. We would write programs in BASIC on punch cards and store them on paper tape. Shortly thereafter, my family got a Commodore PET. My first introduction to code quality came in the form of

```
10 PRINT "ROSS"
20 GOTO 10
```

I was reminded of this when I saw a video of President Barack Obama writing his first line of code at the 2014 Hour of Code event at the White House and wondered if he had the same exciting discovery!

As I moved forward through high school and college, high-quality code meant code that worked. Today, some of the terms I've heard to describe this is "happy path," "daylight scenario," or "get out of bed"—the route through the code under perfect conditions. I think this defines a lot of the early days of "testing" for most people. There is the great story of Grace Hopper and the origin of the term bug. In 1947, she found a flaw that was caused by, literally, a moth stuck in one of the relays and said she had to "debug"—but software testing was very much reactionary.

I joined Microsoft in 1991 in Product Support—literally answering the phones to help people with their problems with Microsoft Works for DOS. I moved to become a software developer in test in 1992, working on a project that would become Windows NT. My job was to write test applications to find bugs. Soon after that, a colleague introduced me to automated tests. I was doing API testing and they suggested that I write some code that would run against each build automatically. I'll never forget my response, "Wow! They let you do that?"—my whole world changed with the introduction to automated testing—and then I went on to build large systems that would run millions of tests over the years.

Things started to change, in my opinion, in 1995, with the introduction of F5. It is not the F5 Networks company, but F5 as the concept of refresh in a browser. Traveling back to the days of the 1960s, 1970s, and 1980s and recalling a company deploying a new software solution, there might be months or years of evaluation, negation, pilots, and training to deploy a new instance of a payroll system. With the rise of the Internet, a new deployment could be as simple as pressing the F5 function key to reload the web page.

I feel we've lived in two parallel worlds since then. On one hand, we have the race for the Internet, building more and more capabilities that can be deployed via a metaphorical F5—CSS, Java, and Flash to concepts like app stores and mobile downloads—and the dominating rise of cloud computing. On the other hand, we have to balance the safety, security, and privacy requirements of enterprise hosted solutions. The deployment of a payroll solution, for example, still takes years of evaluation and training. Many companies are finding the cost savings with cloud solutions offset the security or privacy concerns.

So when it comes to the future of testing, I feel that the days of Big Up-Front Testing (BUFT) are gone forever. I will use Volvo's Concept 26 autonomous car as an example. In the past, no car company in their right mind would ever "outsource" testing the safety of its technology—just as no software developer would allow its users to find a "bug"—for fear of a poor reputation for quality.

However, today's connected world brings together users who want to "help" with companies who need feedback on their services. If Volvo came to you, dear reader, and offered you a free US $45,000 car in return for collecting telemetry data about your experience, would you be willing to sign up?

The joke is that if you don't understand the business model of a web service, look in the mirror. The days of BUFT are gone. That's not to say that customers no longer care about software quality. I believe that software quality will be a huge differentiator. The company that builds an autonomous car that crashes because of a software bug will lose out to the company that has reliable software. The change, I think, will be in the methodology by which companies shape the quality of the software. Instead of hiring armies of testers to try to "test the quality in" to the code, the most creative and innovative companies will develop techniques to motivate and encourage real users to generate the data that help them make quality-related investments.

As we move to a fully connected, mobile world, where F5 "deployment" is the new normal, I think the discipline of "software testing" shifts running a bunch of up-front tests to being savvy in motivating users to generate quality and experiential data that inform the product team and their investments.

The world is changing—in a positive way—and we are open to a future that will allow technology to literally change lives. The old-school equivalent of a "test matrix"—the list of all possible combinations to test ahead of release—is no longer calculable (from hardware to network to operating system to user persona); there are way too many options to enumerate and, therefore, literally impossible to test things up front.

The future of test lies in the world of prediction. Using historical and real-time data to build models to predict where quality-related investments must be made, where support costs will be incurred, and how to use customer feedback from one to improve the experience of another, these systems need to be built and react real time—and the most successful companies of the twenty-first century will be those that can connect with the quality of their customer experiences and respond immediately. It's not possible anymore to test up front—response time is the new normal.

Rahul Viswaroop's Input

Rahul has been with Adobe for 16 years and has experience of managing million-dollar revenue earning desktop products and cloud-hosted services. Currently, Rahul is the quality leader for the Creative Cloud Experience team in Adobe India. He has worked on industry-leading products such as Photoshop, InDesign, Illustrator, PageMaker, After Effects, and Premiere Elements in the past.

He has presented at conferences such as QAI as well as various internal Adobe forums and won awards for his paper presentations. Rahul has a degree in architecture from the Pune University and is the first ISTQB certified tester in India.

Software testing has come a long way in the last two decades. From being an afterthought, to a nice-to-have function, to being an integral part of software development, it is indeed a critical part while building any product or service. The skills expected of test engineers have also changed with time. Test engineers' toolbox has some basic skills that remain true even today. These include customer focus, strong debugging and troubleshooting insights, critical thinking skills, knowledge of scripting languages, programming skills, and understanding of the domain, among others. Along with these prerequisites, one needs to build on the skills that are the need of the hour. While it is impossible to predict the future in its entirety, given the dynamic landscape, here's my attempt to collate the technology roadmap and associated challenges for test engineers in the year ahead.

Awareness of Touch Interfaces and How They
Impact Usability and Performance

With the increased focus on touch interfaces, knowledge of testing applications built for them is critical. This requires unique approaches to validate functionality. The touch surfaces range all the way from being as small as a watch or as large as a coffee table. All leading companies such as Microsoft and Apple are investing in this area and it is set to only explode further in the coming years. Along with the user experience for the two-dimensional workflows, haptic touch adds another dimension of complexity that one has to keep in mind.

Mobile First Workflows

This requires a change in mind-set and tools being used. As mobile penetration increases and more individuals start using multiple mobile devices, the workflows will change completely from the way we know them today. Test engineers need to be able to validate these new workflows.

Reliance on Community and Social Platforms to Solicit Feedback Proactively

The days of shipping products across the fence and waiting for a few weeks or months to receive user feedback are long gone. With the instant reach of social media, reaction to new versions of applications is instantaneous. Test engineers should not only rely on technical support teams to parse this feedback but also bring in individual due diligence with the abundance of information available today. Such a responsive engineering team leaves a positive impression on the company and product. Another aspect testers should consider here is to leverage easy outreach to customers as a tool to either selectively roll out services and gauge feedback or conduct A/B tests with control groups.

Agility in Release Cycles

Traditional release cycles of many months or years have compressed to releasing more frequently.

Agile companies like Facebook release updates to their site multiple times during a day. This requires test engineers to be nimbler in their processes, more judicious about tests to be conducted, and more savvy in taking on calculated risks; all of these while ensuring quality of shipping applications are high. Shorter release cycles lead to challenges like lesser dedicated time for testing. Robust application design, testability of written code, and high bar for quality of code need to be enforced to be able to deliver quality software.

Compressed Duration for Endgame Certification

Applications with a large code base need a dedicated window for integration testing. In projects with annual or greater release cycles, this was easily doable. With multiple frequent releases, this window is now compressed. Test engineers need to identify the base set of tests they will execute. Reliable automation is a must. Focused testing on the areas of code impacted in a particular release should be done. Any risks identified during this testing should be duly highlighted and followed up on.

Connected Workflows

Gone are the days where software applications had isolated footprints. Almost every application has a reach outside the core desktop or mobile primary interface. Desktop products are connected to mobile devices and vice versa.

Mobile apps rely on services to deliver value to users. Test engineers need to understand all the possible touch points of the application they are validating and perform tests that cover all those scenarios. There are many variables and a failure can emanate from any one of the connections. Test engineers need to factor these appropriately at the planning phase itself.

Security

Security breaches and the cost of resultant failures are detrimental to a company's scenarios. There are many variables and of those is an important aspect for test engineers to build skills—this is now more important than ever. Industry acknowledged certifications and best practices should be studied and implemented as a part of the software development process. Security isn't the responsibility of just software security teams. Test engineers especially can help highlight issues by including tests specifically around security in the test plan.

Wearable Technologies

Wearable technologies are set for a huge growth this year. Gaming consoles and fitness devices and tools for specially abled individuals are now becoming more sophisticated. Testing these devices and applications requires a good understanding of the intended use. Since some of these technologies are cutting edge, there may not be existing benchmarks to compare with. A fine balance between testing on simulators and actual devices has to be drawn and one cannot completely replace the other. Test engineers are encouraged to be comfortable in handling and using these devices like a user would in the real-world scenarios.

Internet of Things

With the increase in applications built of the concept of "Internet of Things" (IOT), the testing of these is an aspect that test engineers should be well versed with. Use of common household appliances like washing machines or refrigerators already adopting these technologies means testers need to combine the application of these devices with the technology backbone that supports their "smartness." Since these appliances are in the home and all-pervasive, security testing and privacy settings are paramount and should be prioritized over other forms of testing.

Another example of IOT that is set for an explosion in adoption is driverless cars. This concept is being actively tested in many countries and is set to redefine our concept of owning cars, driving them, and will lead to a new world that we can barely imagine right now. How to test for scenarios for technology that is still taking shape and with applications that can widely vary depending on the nuances of local geography and demographics will be interesting.

DevOps

The lines between traditional IT teams and engineering organizations are blurring due to the nature of connected services and applications. It is difficult to imagine a stand-alone application today that doesn't rely on back-end operations to support it. DevOps is a great career move for test engineers. In agile application development world, the turnaround time to design, develop, test, and deploy is shrinking and having an engineer who is well versed with test methodologies is an asset to the operations team. Yes, there are skills one needs to build around tools being used for this function for configuration management, virtualization, app servers, and web servers, but the transition can be easily done. Since DevOps is still an upcoming field, there is a huge demand for good engineers in this field and should be actively considered by test engineers.

I'll end my piece by saying that a trait every test engineer needs to have is the ability to dream. Often in our urge to be quantitative, we lose the edge on thinking out of the box and be creative in approach to test engineering.

Concluding Thoughts Summarizing the Sentiments of All Three Experts

In summary of what these experts have had to say, I wanted to highlight a few core takeaways on this question of "where are we heading?"

1. The days of BUFT are going away. That said, testing still needs to be up front. It just cannot and need not always be big.

2. Compatible test matrices cannot be fully envisioned and tested for up front, by just an internal test team. The testers will have to spearhead the effort in unison with end users who are also brought in as testers.

3. The experience in coding makes a tester even better.

4. As a tester, you need not do it all. You have several other entities that are also taking part in a quality effort. You need to manage commitments as a tester to get the job done at the end of the day.

5. Continuous delivery will become the norm and not the exception in moving forward.

6. As testers, you will increasingly work toward helping teams innovate and build a competitive advantage.

Did You Know?

1. I have always been interested in short reads that are current and help me connect with the latest in the industry. Given that in this chapter we focus on inputs from veterans and experts in the industry, I have also herein called out such interesting and short reads that will be useful for you, in planning your road ahead:

   a. How agile has changed testing for the good—https://www.techwell.com/techwell-insights/2015/11/testing-isnt-dead-agile-has-changed-it-good

   b. Quality in quantity and how quality is everyone's responsibility—https://www.techwell.com/techwell-insights/2015/11/quality-quantity-how-app-quality-now-everyone-s-responsibility

   c. Where are we heading with manual testing—https://www.techwell.com/techwell-insights/2015/10/it-time-say-goodbye-manual-testing

   d. Software testing as a social responsibility—https://www.techwell.com/techwell-insights/2015/09/software-testing-social-responsibility

   e. Why automated testing will never replace manual testing—https://www.techwell.com/techwell-insights/2015/08/why-automation-will-never-replace-manual-testing

   f. Moving into a world of conscious quality—https://www.techwell.com/techwell-insights/2015/12/moving-world-conscious-quality

References

1. In Tom's article

   Peter F. Drucker, The new realities.

   Fernando Flores, Conversations for action and collected essays (instilling a culture of commitment in working relationships).

   Peter J. Denning and Robert P. Dunham, The innovator's way (successful practices for successful innovation).

2. Ross's book on *Practical Guide to Defect Prevention* is available at: https://www.amazon.com/Practical-Defect-Prevention-Developer-Practices/dp/0735622531.

Index